WHITE MONTH'S RETURN
Mongolia Comes Of Age

WHITE MONTHS RETURN

MONGOLIA COMES OF AGE

Guy Hart

The Book Guild Ltd.
Sussex, England

The Book Guild Ltd.
25 High Street,
Lewes, Sussex

First published 1993
© Guy Hart 1993
Set in Baskerville
Typesetting by Raven Typesetters
Ellesmere Port, South Wirral
Printed in Great Britain by
Antony Rowe Ltd.
Chippenham, Wiltshire.

A catalogue record for this book
is available from the British Library

ISBN 0 86332 875 X

CONTENTS

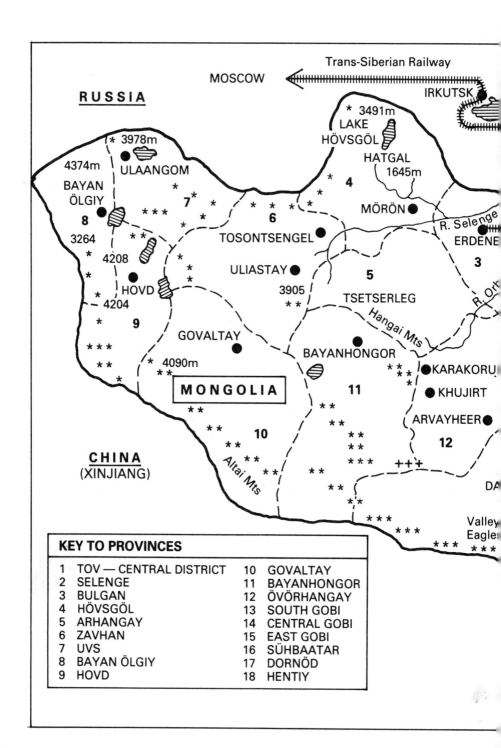

Trans-Siberian Railway

MOSCOW ←⊢⊢⊢⊢⊢⊢⊢⊢⊢⊢⊢⊢⊢⊢⊢⊢⊢⊢⊢⊢⊢⊢⊢⊢⊢⊢⊢ IRKUTSK

RUSSIA

* 3491m
LAKE
HÖVSGÖL

HATGAL
1645m

* 3978m
4374m
ULAANGOM

4

BAYAN
ÖLGIY

7

MÖRÖN

8

6

R. Selenge

3264

TOSONTSENGEL

ERDENE

4208

ULIASTAY

5

3

3905

TSETSERLEG

R. Or

HOVD

4204

9

GOVALTAY

Hangai Mts

BAYANHONGOR

KARAKORU

MONGOLIA

4090m

11

KHUJIRT

ARVAYHEER

10

12

CHINA
(XINJIANG)

Altai Mts

+++

DA

Valley
Eagle

KEY TO PROVINCES

1	TOV — CENTRAL DISTRICT	10	GOVALTAY
2	SELENGE	11	BAYANHONGOR
3	BULGAN	12	ÖVÖRHANGAY
4	HÖVSGÖL	13	SOUTH GOBI
5	ARHANGAY	14	CENTRAL GOBI
6	ZAVHAN	15	EAST GOBI
7	UVS	16	SÜHBAATAR
8	BAYAN ÖLGIY	17	DORNÖD
9	HOVD	18	HENTIY

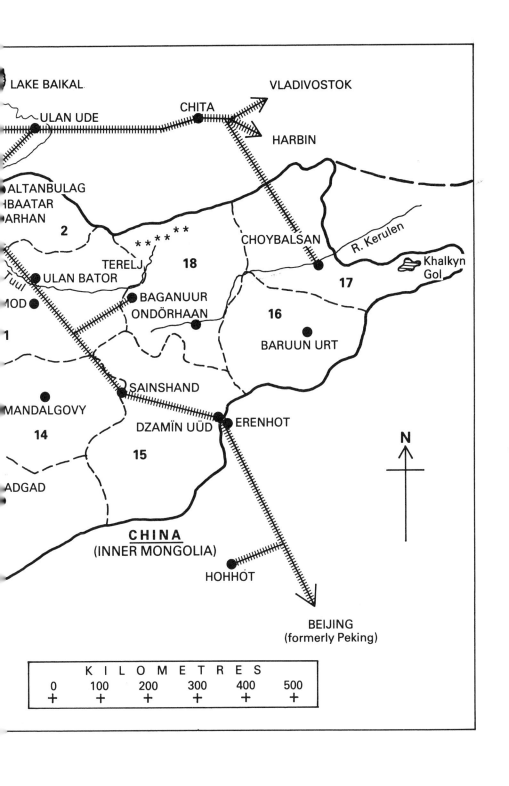

Mongolia fascinated me in anticipation; in materialisation; in retrospect; and most of all in the prospect of going back – some day.

Beatrix Bulstrode, *A Tour in Mongolia*, Methuen, London, 1920

INTRODUCTION

'Tsagaan Sar' (White Month) is the Mongolian Lunar New Year; the first day of spring, according to the old Mongolian almanac. Throughout the ages the festival had been celebrated in the traditional way, particularly in the renewing of family ties and in the honouring of the elderly. However, it was yet another tradition which, after the revolution in Mongolia in 1921, had to be changed in character and purpose or be swept away altogether. In the capital and other urban centres of Mongolia, White Month Festival was therefore virtually discarded in favour of Soviet-style New Year's Eve. Country people, however, in their remoteness yet closeness to nature, clung on to their traditions; but they too were obliged to bend. In the country areas, White Month was transformed into the Spring Festival of Herdsmen – to suit the authorities' collectivisation purposes.

As *glasnost* spread from the then Soviet Union, so the Mongolians began to rediscover all those aspects of their way of life that had been suppressed during their long subservience to Soviet-style Communism. So it was that, in 1989, the Mongolians, town-dwellers and country folk alike, were able to celebrate the Lunar New Year for the first time for many years in their traditional way. White Month's return was like the re-emergence of the White Moon itself after six decades behind the clouds, promising a brighter future. In its way, it was symbolic of all the refreshing changes which started to restore the dignity of the Mongolians.

The Mongols arose out of nowhere in a world-shaking surge to conquest and vast empire. When their force eventually spent itself, the once mighty Mongols experienced steady decline into oblivion, degradation and foreign domination and, eventually, sovietisation which brought progress, yet at the cost of considerable suffering and total subservience. But the world around the Mongolians was set for change, and they, too, caught the first glimpse of a brighter future. Against such a background, it was for me a privilege and an inspiration to spend two years among such enigmatic yet delightful people as the Mongolians at such a momentous turning-point in their long history.

Meanwhile, the world has indeed changed around us all, and Mongolia has moved towards multi-party democracy and a market economy. Inevitably, new stresses and hardships were bound to accompany such a

11

fundamental transition, but the Mongolians' destiny is at long last now in their own hands. In the event, White Month's promise was no delusion.

1

Journey into the Blue

The sun was shining brilliantly in the legendary blue Mongolian sky as we climbed down from the train. On the platform, the Mongolian Chief of Protocol, black Homburg perched on silvery mane, was waiting to greet us. His face, with the long slanting forehead, the aquiline nose and the skin drawn tightly over angular cheekbone, was almost classically American Indian (Mongolians with Eskimo or American Indian features reflect the migration in early times across the Bering Straits). Although the Chief of Protocol really spoke only Mongolian and Russian, his greeting in English, 'How do you do. So nice to see you,' was but one of the twenty-odd versions that he could deploy in various foreign languages. He then introduced us to all the ambassadors and their wives who, according to the local custom, had come to welcome their new colleague and his wife.

Our journey to the land of blue skies, via Hong Kong and Peking, had taken us eight days. It would have been more direct for us to have travelled to Mongolia via Moscow; but that would have involved a twenty-four hour stopover in the transit hotel of Moscow's Sheremetyevo Airport. *Moscow Nights* may have inspired a very popular melody; but a night at the Moscow Airport's transit hotel was then a delight well worth missing. In any case, travelling via Hong Kong and Peking, we had been able to focus on Mongolia, from the outset, as an oriental country and not merely as the seemingly sixteenth republic of the Soviet Union. In the two years ahead of me, I was to find that the Mongolians appreciated the British inclination to regard their country from, as it were, a Far-eastern point of view, and not as the mere extension of the Soviet Union that in many ways it still was. In any case, travelling via Hong Kong and Peking, we avoided too sudden an exposure to a totally different climate and way of life. Even so, in Peking, as we stocked up with fresh vegetables and fruit, etc., the realisation struck home that for the next two years we would just have to do without many things which were regarded as virtually essential in our world. Yet no such thought could detract from our excitement when it came to boarding the 'Peking–Ulan Bator–Moscow' International train on the final stage of our journey. Today, years later, there is a regular scheduled air service between Beijing and Ulan Bator. Moreover, the International Train has recently become something of a travelling market, with entrepreneurial Chinese packing even the corridors with goods to sell whenever the train stops at the numerous stations in Russia on the journey to Moscow. Sordid punch-ups and worse, as disputes arise during the short stops between Chinese traders aboard the train and Russians eager for consumer goods along the track, are spoiling one of the world's great train journeys. But for us, the journey was still a memorable experience. The de-luxe soft class compartment to which the Chinese steward showed us was all wood-panelling, antimacassars, lace curtains and ornate lamps, making for a sense of stepping back in time. However, the (once a week) 7.40 departure time was promptly marked by a lurch and then by a second before the train started to roll forward on its long journey – for us, merely thirty hours to Ulan Bator, as against the six days for the entire journey to Moscow.

The March sun shone thinly through the haze over Beijing as the train picked up speed. We crossed numerous bridges and gazed at the long avenues below, crammed with lorry and bus traffic. There was activity everywhere; and even odd little clearings were filled with elderly Chinese doing their slow motion morning exercises. Thirty minutes later, the train stopped at Nan Kou to take on an extra locomotive for the steep pull up the mountains.

As we climbed, the scenery – though still colourless in March – became more attractive. The stunted trees and bushes on the angular mountain slopes looked exactly like a willow-pattern design. At Qinglonqiao (Dark blue dragon bridge) the train did an inverted Y manoeuvre into the little cul-de-sac station, which involved switching the locomotives to the other end of the train. This gave us five minutes to stretch our legs on the platform, and that was where we had our first real sight of Chang Cheng – the Great Wall of China. I can never quite bring myself to believe the claim that it is the only man-made feature visible from space (what about the Suez and Panama canals?) but the Great Wall is nevertheless truly a breathtaking sight – climbing steeply here, disappearing over a peak, then reappearing there, and so on and on, like some enormous dragon weaving its way across the land.

China has long extended hundreds of miles to the north of the wall, but the wall, started in the third century BC, was built to keep out the marauding bands from the north. In a sense, it served as a boundary between two totally different and opposed ways of life – to the south, the cultured Chinese way of settlement and cultivation; to the north, the restlessness of wild nomadic tribes – the 'soft' life bordering the 'hard' way. Near Qinglonqiao is a town called Zhangjiakou, formerly known as Kalgan and called Khaalga in Mongolian, meaning the gate leading out.

14

Apart from the climb over the mountains, the journey between Beijing and Datong took us through intensively cultivated areas, but as we headed north after leaving Datong the country became increasingly hard, dry and poor. That desolate land was not only so bleak to European eyes, it was also a different world after the bustle and the multitudes of Hong Kong and Beijing. And as our journey progressed we could see that, outside, it was getting colder and colder.

Fourteen hours after leaving Beijing our train pulled into the Chinese border town of Erlian (or Erenhott). As the train stopped at the station, the building was lit up like a Christmas tree and a Viennese waltz was blasting out from the loudspeakers. After our passports had been collected, we were told that we could get out if we wished to and that it would be over two hours before the train departed. Wanting some exercise after the long journey, we put on warm clothing and stepped outside – to a temperature of minus 25°C. The train was then shunted off to have its Chinese, standard-gauge wheels changed for the broader Russian-gauge wheels. Ninety minutes later, the train returned on the outer set of rails. An enormous Chinese steam engine was attached to the front, and we reboarded. Finally, with a piercing but evocative multi-tone whistle, the engine huffed and puffed like some fiery dragon, its steam billowing in the icy night air, and the train made its way out of China for the Mongolian border station of Dzamïn Uüd, fifteen minutes away. As Khaalga denoted the gate out, so *üüd* or *ude* meant the gate in, or entrance. For me, this was the point of entry to my new post as Her Majesty's Ambassador to the Mongolian People's Republic.

At the very neat border station, our passports were examined by a Mongolian border guard who was as smartly turned out as a Grenadier guardsman. I nodded when he asked ' 'Chin said?' (Ambassador?), and the accompanying customs officer passed on. Our Chinese steam engine, which had been decoupled, huffed and puffed its way back across the border, to be replaced at the head of our train by a giant Mongolian double diesel locomotive. At 1.45 in the morning the train set off on the last stage of our journey, and we were finally able to climb into our bunks. At 1.30 the following afternoon our train pulled into the main station at Ulan Bator. As we stepped down, a Mongolian in a black Homburg stepped forward.

2

Arrival in the Back of Beyond

Despite the bright sun, no one lingered in the intense cold after our arrival at the main station. With the introductions to the other ambassadors and to members of our own Embassy swiftly completed, all made a frantic dash for the warmth of their cars. Like the other drivers, Sonom – who was to be my driver – had kept his engine running. As I write, Sonom is now the driver of the Mongolian Ambassador in London. For me, he was an excellent driver, yet it is difficult to imagine that quiet Mongolian negotiating his way around Hyde Park Corner in the rush hour. No doubt he is taking all that in his stride. However, after our arrival, Sonom opened the car door and we climbed in. Years earlier, as a young diplomat, I had joked that those diplomats who ended up in Outer Mongolia presumably spent a good deal of their time trying to convince their colleagues that they really had not transgressed in some way. In the event, I can only say that it was a very moving experience to sit, for the first time, behind the Ambassador's flag with the Royal cipher at its centre, at the very beginning of two fascinating years in Mongolia. But, despite the elation of that moment, I could not have guessed at that stage just how very special Mongolia and its people would become to me.

As we drove through Ulan Bator for the first time, the afternoon sunshine was yielding to a cold, blue light. People clad in thick furs were hurrying about on the pavements, and, in the icy air, vehicles trailed long plumes of steam from their exhausts. After a ten minute drive, we turned off the long Enkh Taivny Gudamzh (Peace Street) into the British Embassy compound.

The main building of the Embassy was a two-storey one, with three staff flats on the ground floor for the other three embassy couples; upstairs, our Residence was on one side and the chancery offices on the other. It was not just that the residence was to be our home for the next two years, the Embassy, of which we made up the fourth married couple, was a family in a very specific and unusual way. At the time, apart from a British Council lecturer at the State University and his French counterpart, we eight were the only Westerners resident in Mongolia. But any eight people who had to live and work together all day and every day for two years in the one building would find it a strain. That my wife and I enjoyed our time in Mongolia so much was due in no small measure to the harmony and sheer fun of living and working with the other couples, everyone of whom we remember so warmly. In harsher times, the posting to Ulan Bator had been described as two years' solitary in a very distant and isolated place with the coldest of winter climates. Although I never saw it that way, we did nevertheless have to face up very quickly to a uniquely different way of life. For example, I was promptly advised to place my order soon for drinks and other bulk supplies – to cover a whole year. Weather conditions on the Trans-Siberian railway from Moscow could be so harsh that insurance would only cover goods shipped in May to arrive in July. It was not easy to work out our own requirements for a whole year, let alone what we would need for over a thousand guests that we estimated we would have to entertain over so long a period. If I mention Mongolian words like *oondook* (eggs), *tooms* (potatoes), *songiin* (onions) and *talkh* (bread), it is merely to give some idea of the strange new words we had to learn. All the assistants spoke Russian in the Delguur shops, but we seemed to get a better loaf when we asked for *talkh* rather than *khleb* – that is, when we used Mongolian and not Russian.

Inevitably, settling in involved learning to live with quite specific hardships, but these were very quickly put into perspective as we took in the beauty and sheer interest of Mongolia. The beauty was all the more striking after the ugliness of the so-called spring. As the snow receded, or (as it seemed) merely evaporated in the driest of atmospheres, the colourless land looked utterly dead. It was at this time, when the country looked as if it had finally given up the ghost, that the spring winds raged, driving the dry earth up into stifling dust storms which lacerated the eyes of man and beast. One almost asked aloud why it was that God had forsaken this land.

One Sunday, after the dust storms had died away, we were sitting on the dry earth of a hillside when, suddenly, we noticed a patch of intense violet. The pulsatilla, pasque flower, was our first sight of returning life. In the week that followed, clumps of yellow, blue and crimson iris shot up. Towards the end of May the first rains fell, and the transformation was almost unbelievable in its suddenness and extent. The grasslands, the birches and larches turned a bright green, and the profusion of wild flowers was so great that it was almost impossible to avoid stepping on an edelweiss here or a gentian there. By mid-June, with intermittent showers, the grass was knee high, and the warming sun brought out the scents of wild flowers and herbs such as thyme. The defrozen rivers babbled and swirled rapidly over ancient rocks, and in the crystal-clear waters Arctic char and grayling rose to take flies on the surface.

In a world of increasingly less 'natural' nature, few countries can match the unspoilt beauty of Mongolia. Although it is a country roughly the size of Western Europe, it has a population of just two million, and much of its rugged and awe-inspiring vastness has been untouched by man. Moreover, it is a very varied land – from the flat Gobi in the south, the seemingly endless grasslands of the steppe which merge into the wooded hills in the north and, beyond, the taiga region bordering on Siberia itself, to the High Altai mountains hemming in the country in the west. Then, in addition to the 25 million national herd of horses, camels, yaks, cows, reindeer, sheep and goats, the wild life is abundant and varied from snow leopards, saiga antelopes and marmots to steppe eagles and cranes. Finally, it is an ancient land with dinosaur remains and cave paintings, as well as substantial mineral deposits.

Although of different origins, there are more Mongols living in Inner Mongolia in China and in Russia than in Mongolia itself, yet Mongolia is the Mongol heartland.

Who, then, are the people of this heartland?

Unspoilt beauty of Mongolia. High summer in the river Tuul valley.

Buddha and Stupa at the Gandan Monastery, Ulan Bator.

Lake Hubsugul, cold but pristine and awe-inspiring beauty. Over 260 metres deep, the lake holds the world's third largest quantity of fresh water.

A herdswomen in Zavhan with her Bactrian camel.

Boy rider and marshal at Naadam, the annual games of the three ancient Mongol sports of horse racing, wrestling and archery.

At the onset of winter, only the edges of the swiftly flowing rivers are fringed with ice.

Ice field. In spring, no sooner does the snow melt in the bright sun, than it freezes.

The residence, with its holy gate, of the former Bogd Khan, the corrupt pronunciation of which became the name 'Urga' by which Ulan Bator was known prior to 1924.

3

The Mongols

The Mongols and their homelands are still so comparatively unknown to the rest of the world that the very mention of 'Outer Mongolia', if now mistakenly, is nevertheless still widely used – particularly to imply extreme remoteness. In a way, the Mongols have always been a secret people. Their first chronicle, written between 1228 and 1240, was called *The Secret History of the Mongols*, (*Nuuts Tovchoo*). No one is certain about the origin of the name Mongol, or exactly what it meant. Moreover, the Mongols were assigned a variety of incorrect names by those who feared them, ranging from Huns and Tartars to Barbarians. Something of the fear and, indeed, sheer horror that they inspired, centuries ago, comes through to us today in our word 'horde', taken from the Mongolian *ordu* (camp).

Despite the veritable beauty of Mongolia, which is reflected in the Mongolians' love of nature as well as in their songs, poetry and literature, the country – with its harsh and extreme climate – can also be a cruel and unrelenting one. Even today, Mongolia's great distances and vast open spaces convey an awe-inspiring sense of emptiness. As one horizon rolls into the next, the stark beauty seems devoid of gentleness. In such a place, the Mongols existed in earlier times as relatively small clans, living, through their animals, off the land and off weaker tribes. Such an existence was a constant challenge. It was also a constantly changing pattern of alliances and strife between the tribes, to the extent that, at that stage, the Mongols did not really constitute a united nation. All that was to change – and the world was to know about it.

In 1162 a son, Temujin, was born to the khan of the Yakka Mongols. When, thirteen years later, his father was poisoned by Tartars, Temujin endeavoured, with his mother's help, to establish himself as khan. He succeeded; but to put it that briefly is to skate over what was a remorseless testing time, which included capture by rivals and subsequent escape and the imposition of his iron will and flair. Thereafter, Temujin sought to unite the various clans and, by 1194, he became known as Genghis Khan (Lord of the Universe). Acknowledged by the Kuriltai (council) in 1206 as Khaghan, or Khan of Khans, Genghis Khan called his tribes 'the Mongols'. In 1211 he invaded China, the Mongol hordes breaking through the Great Wall to Peking. Then it was the turn of Afghanistan and Persia, before Genghis Khan died in 1227. He was succeeded by his son Ogadei, who, in 1235, built the first Mongol city, Karakorum. Another son, Batu, Khan of the Golden Horde, dominated the Lower Volga region and took Moscow and Kiev. One of Genghis Khan's grandsons became the first of the ilkhans in Persia, and another, Kublai, established himself as the first emperor of all China, setting up the Yuan dynasty in the process. The Mongol empire stretched from the Sea of Japan to Egypt and the borders of Hungary, from Siberia to the Strait of Malacca. But what had blown up like an irresistible Mongolian dust storm had spent itself. When Ogadei died in 1241, Batu, Khan of the Golden Horde in the west, returned to Karakorum and never ventured west again. Kublai, who was so fascinated with China that he became sinicised, remained in China until his death in 1294. In 1368 his Yuan dynasty was overthrown by the Ming, and thereafter the Ming attacked the Mongol heartland, destroying its capital, Karakorum, in 1398.

It is surely amazing that Genghis Khan and his Mongols, in their remoteness and relatively primitive condition, could have known so much about the outside world to think of taking it on in the first place. It is even more amazing that such people succeeded to the extent that they did. From the outset, Genghis Khan had understood that allegiance to a tribal chief rested on his ability to provide the spoils which flowed from conquest. Other chiefs also understood this. Yet it was an insatiable fire of ambition within him, of reaching out for the universe, as well as a seemingly invincible singlemindedness, that set him above all others. He also understood his Mongols. Their wild homeland had made them hardy and tough. They were superb horsemen and archers; and they were cunning, seemingly fearless, and cruel.

The restless Mongols burst out of their open spaces, with all the abandon of those unencumbered by worries about protecting possessions, to hurl themselves at and to break through the patterns elsewhere of settled and cultivated life. Thereafter, they added to their strength and experience by deploying the technologies, material and manpower resources which accrued from each victory in succeeding onslaughts. This practice of progressively adding captured manpower to their forces, thereby uprooting group after group, surely amounted to a very considerable and significant stirring of the human pot. However, the Mongols were not always successful; the very first use by the Japanese of kamikaze suicidal tactics thwarted the Mongols' attempt to cross the Sea of Japan. Nevertheless, as the hordes moved west they increasingly became a mighty war machine, an irresistible force with, seemingly, no immovable obstruction in its various paths. Inevitably, however, they became over-extended, and with each advance the hordes became more racially disparate. In any case, the Mongols had no civilisation or culture to impart. The earlier observation of Genghis Khan's Chinese adviser, that what had been won from the saddle could not be ruled from the saddle, was as valid after others had succeeded Genghis Khan. So the Mongols' power ebbed and, with leadership and tribal disputes, their decline set in.

Batmonkh, in the first half of the sixteenth century, was the last khan of the Mongol nation. In view of the vast, wide-open spaces in which the Mongols lived, it is amazing that Genghis Khan managed to unite the tribes in the first place. But it is the more understandable that, with decline and leadership disputes feeding on each other, a process had started that could only lead to the break-up of what might be called greater Mongolia. This process had been matched and spurred on by the growth of Manchu power. It seems that this growth encouraged the Mongols to extend their existing links with Tibet, just as much as did an affinity between the Mongols and the Tibetans. The Mongol–Tibetan connection led to the introduction of Lamaist-Buddhism into Mongolia and in the late sixteenth century, when the chief Tibetan Lama visited Mongolia, he was called – for the very first time – Dalai Lama by the Mongols. A few years later, the first Buddhist monastery in Mongolia was built at Erdene Dzuu, immediately adjacent to the site of the former Karakorum.

A few years earlier, Hohhot (Blue Town) had been built in what is now Inner Mongolia. But the time of greater Mongolia had just ended, and Inner Mongolia was swamped by the Manchus. As the Manchus conquered Peking and their Ching dynasty replaced the Ming, Inner Mongolia was increasingly colonized and drawn in as the part of China that it remains to this day. That is not to say that the Manchus ignored Outer Mongolia. On the contrary, they took control of the country, ruling over it from the old trading centre of Uliastay in Western Mongolia. The proud and once mighty Mongols lost political power, and thus their independence. The khan system was eroded, eventually to fall away. The keeping alive of the Outer Mongolian sense of national identity therefore revolved around Lamaism and, in particular, around the khutukhtu (he who is blessed), the top ranking Mongolian incarnation, lower only to the Dalai and Panchen Lamas. This identifying of the faith with the nation was to have lasting effect. However, although the Manchus' control over Outer Mongolia was substantial, they did not acquire the lasting hold over the country that they achieved over Inner Mongolia. In this a key factor was Outer Mongolia's bordering with Russia. The extension of the tsarist Russian border to the River Amur coincided with a waning of Manchu Chinese control, and to some extent Outer Mongolia became a Russian protectorate.

In 1911, the Outer Mongolians declared themselves independent; and the khan system was restored, with the Khutukhtu becoming secular head as well, the first (and only one) to be called Bogd Khan (Holy Chief). However, Mongolian independence was not recognised by China or, as it transpired, by Russia, the latter conceding in 1913 that Outer Mongolia was an autonomous part of China. In any case, in the aftermath of the Russian Revolution in 1917, Russian influence in the Far East weakened and the Chinese promptly moved back to restore their rule over Outer Mongolia.

By the beginning of the twentieth century, the population had dwindled to half a million. Forty per cent of the male population were lamas, and the remainder were almost totally uneducated and without health care. The Mongols' nomadic life of roaming free as the wind and with pride and daring had become, by the dawn of the twentieth century, a mean, subsistence existence with no enlightenment save for their faith. Foreign rule, which had isolated the Mongols, as well as abuse by some lamas and Mongolian landowners, had locked the Mongols, as it were, in the Middle Ages. Beatrix Bulstrode's heartrending account, in her book *A Tour in Mongolia*, of prisoners incarcerated for life in coffin-like boxes whereby 'death is indisputably preferable to imprisonment in Mongolia', was written not in the era of Genghis Khan but in 1913.

Could it be that, just as the Tibetans had ceased to be a warlike race with their conversion to Buddhism in the sixth century, the Mongols became submissive after Lamaism (with its teaching of immediate reincarnation) arrived in Mongolia? In any event, the Mongolians had been caught up in changing patterns of power play between Russia, China – with Japan set to pursue its own interests. The Soviet Revolution inspired hope in some Mongolians that life in Outer Mongolia could be changed, and approaches were made to the Soviets. The latter were not disinterested (particularly in the development of Mongolian party cells), but were at the time doubtless primarily concerned with consolidating their own revolution, particularly in the face of widespread hostility abroad. In the event, it was a former tsarist officer, Baron von Sternberg, who, encouraged by the Japanese, moved with his motley bands into Mongolia and eventually drove the Chinese out of Urga. However, any welcome extended to him soon turned to revulsion and horror as the havoc which von Sternberg and his bands went on to wreak exceeded the harshness of Chinese rule. This time there was a direct Soviet interest in the disposing of the motley White Russian band on the loose in Mongolia. In addition, the nucleus of a Mongolian revolutionary party had by this time come into being in exile in the Soviet Union, and revolutionary forces had been recruited. In the spring of 1921 these forces moved into Mongolia, defeating the Chinese on the northern border and opening the way for the establishment of a Mongolian revolutionary government on Mongolian soil at Altan Bulag. Thereafter, Soviet and Mongolian forces went on to occupy Urga on 6 July 1921. Five days later, a People's Revolutionary Government was established in the Mongolian capital. In the meantime, von Sternberg's bands had mutinied and dispersed, von Sternberg being captured and shot by the Soviets.

The ruling Bogd Khan remained head of state on the establishment of the revolutionary government, although his powers were limited, but when he died in 1924 the Mongolian People's Republic was proclaimed. Mongolia was thus the second country in the world to become a Communist state – that is, over two decades before the spread of Communism elsewhere after the Second World War. Lenin saw Mongolia as a model of a country transforming directly from feudalism to Communism without experiencing capitalism.

In 1922 the first prime minister, a lama called Bodo, was shot for 'counter-revolutionary activities'. Sukhe Bator (nowadays spelt 'Süh-baatar'), the hero of the revolution, died in mysterious circumstances in his thirtieth year – rumours persisted that he was poisoned. In his honour, Urga, the capital, was renamed Ulan Bator (Red Hero).

Sukhe Bator was a revolutionary. He had spent some time in the USSR and he wanted something better for his people. But did he and his fellow revolutionaries really want Mongolia to adopt a totally Soviet way of life, to the detriment of the Mongolians' self-respect? He never survived to see the suffering, such as that inflicted on herdsmen in an attempt to force them to accept collectivisation. The Mongolians had been obliged to implement collectivisation roughly in parallel with that process in the USSR. However, historically, the Mongols' nomadic way of life had revolved around and, indeed, had depended on their 'most-treasured possessions', namely, their horses, camels, cows, sheep and goats. As a result the Mongolians had the closest attachment to their animals, and the idea of yielding them up to the collective and of the former owners working (under politically vigilant brigade leaders) in a collective was anathema to them, and was bitterly resisted. In fact, the first attempt at collectivisation led to such resentment and division that collectives were abolished in 1932. It took two decades before the regime was finally able to convince country folk that they would benefit more from working within collectives than by toiling on their own.

However, one of the revolutionaries, Choybalsan, was bent on the sovietisation of Mongolia, and he set about consolidating his hold over the country. If he was indeed driven, in his unswerving loyalty to Stalin, by a desire to avoid Mongolia being absorbed into the Soviet Union, the cruelty of his regime (for much of which he was personally responsible) is nevertheless undeniable. The approach which he adopted on two fronts was systematic and brutal. It was aimed at destroying all those party figures whom he saw as a threat to his ambitions, and at obliterating Buddhism in Mongolia, which he saw as a direct ideological challenge.

In the first half of the 1930s the Japanese held themselves up as both the promoters of pan-Mongolism – to unite the Mongols not just in Mongolia but also in China and the Soviet Union – and the protectors of Buddhism – with the promise to search in Inner Mongolia for the ninth khutukhtu. But the Mongols were only too well aware of the risk of incurring the wrath of both the Soviet Union and China to entertain any such ideas. Nevertheless, this background was very convenient for Choybalsan's purposes. Numerous Mongolian party figures were accused, falsely, of aiding and abetting Japanese imperialism. By the late 1930s Choybalsan was the only senior party figure to have survived the purges.

Meanwhile, the destruction of Buddhism in Mongolia had proceeded apace. Lamaism, with its stand against cultivation and fishing, had been partly responsible for the Mongols' backwardness, and some lamas had indeed been part of the earlier feudal exploitation. Nevertheless, there remained much about Lamaism that the people respected, and their religious faith was still deeply ingrained. Choybalsan subverted this by systematic denigration, and then set about the destruction of hundreds of monasteries and the massacre of thousands of lamas.

By 1939 Choybalsan had become prime minister, and also held several other key portfolios. His position was unassailable – from within Mongolia. But for Stalin's preoccupation with the impending Second World War, Choybalsan, with his own personality cult, might just have been considered to have grown too big for his boots.

In 1939 Soviet and Mongolian forces, under Zhukov's command, defeated an invading Japanese force at Khalkhyn Gol. By 1940 the job of 'building socialism' in Mongolia had begun. In 1945, a plebiscite was held with the aim of achieving Chinese recognition of the Mongolian People's Republic. In the event, this recognition was forthcoming – from the then Kuomintang government.

However, this bolstering of Mongolian independence on the one hand was undermined on the other when, also in 1946, the Russian Cyrillic alphabet was adopted in place of the old Mongolian script. Moreover, on Choybalsan's death in 1952 (the year before the death of his model, Stalin) Tsedenbal's succession as Prime Minister implied continuing loyalty and subservience to the Soviet Union. However, in 1954 Damba ousted Tsedenbal from control of the party; Mongolia's relations with China improved, and Chinese workers started coming to assist with various projects (the Chinese-looking main railway bridge in Ulan Bator was but one of those projects). Moreover, the railway, which in 1949 had linked Ulan Bator to the Trans-Siberian line, was extended south in 1956 to the Chinese border at Erenhot. Mongolia's relations with the People's Republic of China (which had itself come into being in 1949) were proceeding fraternally – to the Mongolians' relief, for the balancing of their relations with their giant neighbours to the north and south had for so long been their major preoccupation. The Twentieth Congress of the Communist Party of the Soviet Union – at which Khrushchev denounced Stalin's personality cult – was to mark a turning point, however. Thereafter, Mongolia's relations with China could not but be affected by the growing disenchantment between the Soviet party and what Mao Tse-tung regarded as his orthodox party. As Sino-Mongolian relations deteriorated, so all the Chinese workers were sent home – in some cases, in mid-project. The Mongolian party chief, Danba, could not survive this about-turn, and in 1958 the Moscow-loyal Tsedenbal recovered control of the Mongolian party – despite the fact that in 1957, under Damba, collectivisation had been reintroduced, more gently and successfully than the first time round in 1931.

In 1962, following the earlier Soviet lead over Stalin, the Mongolian party criticised the personality cult of Mongolia's little Stalin, Choybalsan, and at Soviet insistence the 800th anniversary of Genghis Khan's birth was marked in very low key.

As Choybalsan had been in so many respects a mirror image of Stalin, so Tsedenbal was Mongolia's Brezhnev; but with the passing of the Brezhnev era, so Tsedenbal fell from grace. In 1984 Batmonkh took over as head of state and party, with Sodnom as his prime minister.

Mongolia was not the first Communist country I had served in but, as I had not been in the Soviet Union, Mongolia was the country in which the Communist system was more deeply established than anywhere else I had ever visited. The majority of Mongolians, born after the revolution in 1921, had never known anything but the Communist system. Being so remote geographically and not having anything of relevance in their history that they could draw on, the Mongolians (or so it seemed to me when I first arrived in their country) found it difficult to conceive that there could be a different way of life. They had become sovietised to the extent that I found them far less oriental than I would have expected, and they had come to feel shame where their culture, history and backwardness were concerned. Moreover, the Mongolians were the only other people to suffer all the brutalities that, between the 1920s and the 1970s, the Soviet Union inflicted on its own people. For all that, however, it has to be acknowledged that the Soviet Union did a very great deal, at considerable cost, to develop Mongolia. It is certainly the case that the Soviet Union had mineral extraction and strategic interests in Mongolia, and although Soviet assistance to Mongolia ranked third after its aid to Cuba and Vietnam, it had the element of a direct Soviet border interest. Nevertheless, schools, hospitals, housing – indeed, whole towns where there had been none – plus a standard of living that was arguably higher than the average throughout the Soviet Union were all credits due to the Russians. One may well ask as to the price that the Mongolians had to pay, but it has to be realised that the Mongolians were being squeezed into extinction by feudal oppression before the revolution in 1921. This was entirely different from the circumstances in which the countries of Eastern Europe were absorbed into the then Soviet bloc at the end of the Second World War.

With their long-standing loyalty, even subservience, to the Soviet Union, it was a matter of course that the Mongolians bent with the prevailing wind from Moscow, and they had never questioned any change of direction. When a new Soviet leader, Mikhail Gorbachev, came to power in March 1985, the Mongolians prepared once again to trim their sails. At first, Gorbachev seemed to be saying that there was nothing wrong with the Communist system that a little discipline could not cure and with Mongolia's much longer experience of Communism than that of any of the Eastern European countries, this was a line that the Mongolian leadership could understand. Moreover, when Gorbachev instituted an anti-alcohol drive in the Soviet Union, to instil discipline in an attempt to increase productivity, so Mongolia followed suit. However, as Gorbachev came face to face with the harsh realities of Soviet economic decline (and disasters such as those of Chernobyl and the Aral Sea), he recognised the need for genuine and far-reaching reform.

When I arrived in Mongolia in 1987, the Mongolians were at first utterly bewildered by *glasnost, perestroika* and the New Thinking – all of which seemed directly to contradict so much of what they had so long accepted as gospel. Initially, I was to encounter so many examples of the old-style approach. However, precisely because the Mongolian People's Revolutionary Party had always been the most loyal of all the pro-Moscow Communist parties, once again it bowed to the new line from Moscow. This was to prove a key factor. The democratic opposition which later came into being was largely inspired by subsequent transformations in Eastern Europe. Reform was adopted at the outset, if not particularly sensationally, by the Mongolian People's Revolutionary Party. As changes were implemented, so Mongolia came fourth to Hungary, Poland and the Soviet Union itself on the list of Communist countries carrying out reform – that is to say, Mongolia's reforms were under way when the hard-liners were still in control in the GDR, Czechoslovakia and Bulgaria, and so on. This relatively early start by the Mongolian ruling party was to have further significance later, for when the democratic opposition eventually sprang up the ruling party already held a good deal of the reform high ground. As a result (but also because Mongolia was placed neither by history nor by geography to draw automatically on Western democratic traditions and market economy experience) the Mongolian People's Revolutionary Party was to retain control long after most of its counterparts in other countries had been overthrown.

However, although I spent only two years in Mongolia, the period 1987 to 1989 marked a turning-point for the Mongolians. As they came to comprehend the reality of all the changes in the air, so they gradually understood that Mongolia's independence was at long last to be genuine, with all the opportunities and responsibilities that that implied. I count myself very fortunate to have been in Mongolia at the time when the Mongolians finally started to rediscover themselves.

4

The Ger

The Mongols have by no means been the only nomads in the world. The Masai of Kenya, for example, have traditionally followed a very similar cattle-breeding nomadic way of life, but they have done so in entirely different climatic conditions. The conditions with which the Mongols have had to contend have been extreme, ranging from intense cold in the depth of winter – with raging dust-storms in spring and the occasional earth tremor – to short bursts of summer heat. An architect would have his work cut out to design a dwelling capable of providing for such factors, and he would probably give up altogether if the client were to add the stipulation that the dwelling also had to be capable of being dismantled within an hour for manageable transportation to a distant site for easy re-erection. However, although transportability was an essential require-ment, the dwelling also had to allow for expression of artistry so that it would acquire the feel of a true home. The Mongols, as well as other Asiatic races, found the answer over three thousand years ago in the yurt tent. One factor which worked in their favour was that the tent would not have to withstand, as it could not, a damp climate with prolonged periods of heavy rain. In the relatively dry conditions in Mongolia, the yurt proved ideal over the ages, and it was called, in Mongolian, the *ger* (pronounced 'gair').

Life in Mongolia has changed a great deal. A quarter of the population now lives in Ulan Bator, mainly in recently built apartment blocks, and in other towns and settlements in the country people live in permanent buildings. Mongolia has also become self-sufficient in wheat production. However, arable farming is not extensive, because the needs of so small a population can be met from relatively restricted arable areas; further-more, in the harsh environment and dry conditions found in Mongolia, arable farming can so easily result in soil erosion. But much of Mongolia is covered with grassland, and the main rural occupation remains the rearing of livestock. With constant moves to new pastures the ger remains indispensable. Over and above this, however, even if nomadic life is no longer as widespread as it formerly was, the ger has for so very long played

28

such a key part in the Mongolians' way of life that it is closely bound up with their culture. To know something about the Mongolian ger is better to understand and appreciate the Mongolians themselves.

What, then, is a ger? Briefly, it is a free-standing wooden structure which is covered with felt and canvas, but which has an open top. However, such a short description says nothing about the charm and comfort of a ger.

Herdsmen making frequent changes of summer pasturing often use small gers without any flooring. More usually, however, the first part of assembling a ger is the careful laying of the circular floor, made up of cut boards. Then the doorway (*üüd* or *ude*, as previously mentioned) is positioned, always facing south. Linking up at either side of the door, strips of lattice walling (*khana*) are erected around the edge of the floor. Next comes a large cartwheel-like crownpiece (*toono*) which forms the open top and which is supported by two pillars (*baganas*). The free-standing structure is complete after over a hundred long struts (*unis*) have been attached, like spokes, between the crownpiece-top and the top of the lattice walls. Finally, a layer of felt (with an extra layer in winter) and a canvas top cover are stretched around and over the structure, the sides of the ger being bound round with ropes of hide or horsehair.

A stove is placed in the centre of the ger, with a smokestack extending through the top opening. Fine carpets are laid on the floor and decorative cloth hangings are attached around the lattice side walls. Furniture is located not just in a suitable but, more, in its traditional place – the rear of the tent, facing the door, being the *khoimor*, the place for displaying treasured items and for the seating of honoured guests.

The wooden structure of a ger is often highly decorated, against a background colour of orange or red. All the furniture is similarly coloured and decorated, forming a harmonious whole with the ger. The furniture is specially designed for tent life, with, for example, clothes chests instead of wardrobes, and no space is wasted. Thus, a clothes chest is front-opening, so that its top can serve as a table or working top, and bed-heads contain little drawers, and so on.

With a large open top, the air inside a ger changes all the time, yet the stove ensures that the tent is warm in winter. Moreover, since the door of a ger always faces south, the sunlight entering through the open top makes it possible for one to tell the time in a ger, on the sundial principle. Traditionally, the daylight inside a ger was divided up into periods, like hare-time and horse-time. The early morning's rays showed the time for the milking and pasturing of animals, but if the light shone on to the back of the tent, that is, after midday, it indicated that it was already too late to set off on a long journey. There are numerous other features of the ger. For example, a very large rock is often attached to a rope hanging from the crownpiece top, which helps to prevent the ger from being lifted in high winds. Then, an outer flap can be pulled over the open top in inclement weather. This flap, which is normally rolled to one side of the tent top, is called the *orgoo*. The flap of a chief was often specially decorated, so distinguishing his residence. So it was that the capital of Mongolia was at one time known as 'Orgoo' – or rather, 'Urga', as Russians and other foreigners found it easier to pronounce.

How colourful and evocative it is to hear the Mongolian word 'Gerleku?' being used to enquire if a man is married, the literal question being, 'Have you set up your tent?' (the enquiry 'Mordoku?' of a woman as to whether she is married is on the lines of 'Have you been carried off on horseback?'). When, after my first year in Mongolia, a formal note was sent to the Foreign Ministry in Ulan Bator that I was going on leave to England, the Mongolian translation was that I was returning to my tent in England. So 'ger' means home – but a home as free as the wind itself, and one which, with its essential elements unchanged over the ages, links Mongolians so directly with their roots.

Much as I have admired the fine, upright and proud Masai people of Kenya's Mara region, I could never feel drawn to spending the night in one of their dark and dismal mud huts. But a night spent in a Mongolian ger is sheer delight as one gazes up at the stars or catches the first light of dawn through the tent's open top. And it is a stirring sight to see shining white gers against the green of the steppes, like button mushrooms sprouting on a lawn.

5

The Capital of Mongolia

Since 1924, the capital of Mongolia has been known as Ulan Bator. Originally, the Mongols did not have, let alone build, a capital city, and the various tribes were small and disunited anyway. The first Mongol capital city was Karakorum which was built by Genghis Khan's son, Ogadei. Unlike the Samarkand of Tamerlane, however, it did not survive.

In 1639, the then 5-year-old Zanabazar (who was to become Mongolia's greatest sculptor, of Buddhas cast in gold) was declared spiritual leader. His camp, Shar Bosiyn Orgoo (Yellow Silk Residence) automatically became the Mongolian capital. From its site at the time at Tsagaan Nuur (White Lake), the camp moved twenty times over the next 140 years until, in 1778, it reached and settled at the spot in the valley of the River Tuul which is today Ulan Bator. At first the town was known as 'Grouped Monasteries'; and then as 'Capital Monastery'. But if monasteries were one essential feature, another was the residence of the spiritual leader, and a permanent complex of temples and residence was built. As was mentioned in the previous chapter, 'Orgoo' became the Mongolian word for residence from what might be called the ger culture. Particularly during the period when Mongolia was a virtual tsarist Russian protectorate, the corrupt form 'Urga' was the name by which the Mongolian capital was more widely known until 1924, changing at that revolutionary stage to Ulan Bator.

Will the Mongolians yet again change the name of their capital, when so much else has changed around them? It seems likely, but they can hardly go back to a name which refers to the residence or monastery because that is bound up too much with a harsh feudal past. The 'Bator' they would probably wish to retain in honour of their national hero, Sukhe, but the 'Ulan', which means red, is becoming increasingly irrelevant. An obvious alternative, to give the capital the hero's name 'Sühbaatar' (axe hero), is not feasible, because there is already a town as well as an *aimag* (province) of that name. It will be interesting, therefore, to see what name will eventually replace Ulan Bator. However, one point about the Mongolian capital is unlikely to change: it will surely remain, in winter, the world's coldest capital.

Ulan Bator lies approximately one-third of the way south of the north–south spur of the Trans-Siberian railway, connecting Beijing and Moscow. The surrounding area is hilly – in parts, mountainous even – with forests of larch and birch crowning most hilltops. The hills rise sharply at the edges of the broad valley through which the River Tuul flows on its way to join the Selenge and thence to Lake Baikal. At an altitude of 1350 metres above sea level, and about as distant from the sea as is possible, the atmosphere in Ulan Bator is particularly dry. The dryness makes the long, intensely cold winter and the short hot summer more bearable. The climate is healthy, as long as one wears the right clothing for the right season, although the dry atmosphere can lead at times to a slight feeling of dizziness.

Despite the beauty of the surrounding countryside, Ulan Bator could not be described as a particularly beautiful city. But just to be there makes one feel a significance that can be experienced nowhere else – everything is so very different. There is also a quiet restraint to the Mongolian way of life, and one must frequently look beyond the simplicity to perceive the originality and charm.

The residence and the monastery reflect this simplicity. They are important, not as grand buildings, but as the original *raison d'être* of the city.

The residence is situated at the foot of the sacred mountain, Bogd Üül. It was down the slopes of this mountain that, in 1920, von Sternberg's bands surged to capture the residence and, with it, the city. And until the Bogd Khan Jebtsun Damba Khutukhtu's death in 1924, the residence was where Mongolia's spiritual leader and head of state lived. Today, when it serves merely as a museum, the residence looks much as it did in earlier times. The strange complex of buildings is a mixture of Chinese pavilions and Siberian-type log houses around little courtyards, the one leading into the other. In winter, it can be a fearfully cold place to walk around. Moreover, for me, it had a forlorn feeling, as if it were some discarded stage set. There was nothing to convey any sense of the residence as the former centre of activity, nor was there anything which gave an insight into what it must have been like when von Sternberg's bands broke into it. All that, after the establishment of the Mongolian People's Republic, was virtually taboo. I could only hope that, as the Mongolians settled into their newly genuine independence, they would rediscover their history and culture, and that something as important to them as the residence would become more than a cold and musty museum piece.

Across the valley from the residence stands the main Gandan

Monastery which, in my time in Mongolia, was the only one still functioning in the country. The main building, the Meghjid Janraiseg Temple, rising to a considerable height from the open ground surrounding it, is a striking yet rather gaunt sight. It was built early in the twentieth century by the Chinese. It formerly housed an enormous Buddha which was removed, according to what I heard, to Leningrad after the revolution. This Buddha, one of the largest in the world, is not precisely the sort of symbol to the Mongolians that St Stephen's Crown is to the Hungarians, but its return would be as significant as was the Hungarians' recovery of their treasured crown from its place of safe keeping in the United States. As it is, the main building remains virtually an empty shell. It was therefore in the adjacent Tsogchin Temple that the monastery functioned in my time. However, it seemed to me at that stage that the Mongolians had not yet come to terms with their Buddhist traditions. Mongolian Buddhism originally came from Tibet. However, their early form of Lamaism, precluding the Mongolians from cultivating, fishing (and even, so it was said, from washing), left them locked in a backward state, living under a feudal system. All this, in addition to the harsh foreign rule inflicted on them, was before the revolution. After it had taken place, religion was set for erosion and, later, for obliteration. There was no attempt to search for a replacement Bogd Khan spiritual leader in 1924, monasteries were increasingly closed and destroyed, and many lamas were put to death in the 1930s – in particular, at a gathering at the Mansjir Monastery near Zummod in Central province. In such circumstances, the majority of Mongolia's population, born after 1921, had been taught that Lamaism was part of the exploitation that Mongolia had suffered, and they thus grew up without religion.

Originally, Shamanism had flourished in Mongolia, and it seemed to me, during my time in the country, that just as sailors, up against the elements, tend to be superstitious, so the Mongolians, existing in one of the harshest of environments, reached out for something beyond Marxism–Leninism. On reaching the crest of a hill I frequently found a cairn, called an *oboo*, built up over time by passers-by adding a stone, or an ox-skull, and certain trees would be decorated with strips of cloth and with mongh (cent) coins and matchsticks wedged in bark cracks.

In my time, the very few surviving lamas were very tame and compliant with the system. Indeed, an Asian Buddhist peace organisation in Ulan Bator served the interests of the Soviet bloc's campaign for world peace. However, after the long and widespread persecution of Lamaism in Mongolia, that was perhaps understandable. I shall deal later with the part that Buddhism may come to play in Mongolia's future. All that there was for me to experience were Buddhist temples transformed into museums, like the green-roofed Tibetan-style Choi Jin Sum (the former residence of the Bogd Khan's brother) with all its brutal paintings, and the services at Gandan Monastery.

There was invariably a steady if not a large number of worshippers at the latter. Prayer wheels would be turned, full-length prostrations on special slats and circum-walking of stupas would be performed and pigeons would be fed, while in the background the lamas would chant '*Om mani padme hum*' – 'There is treasure in the lotus' – and a brass gong would sound at regular intervals. The area around the Gandan Monastery, which stands on a hill, was covered with rows and rows of gers, yet the authorities were somehow ashamed of this very Mongolian setting, taking pride, instead, in the prefabricated blocks of workers' flats which, increasingly, were becoming the face of Ulan Bator.

There was also the same unnecessary sense of shame over what was called the Sunday market. For a long time, this was virtually the only private enterprise. Mongolians would take along anything they had to sell, from clothing to rusty nails. Interest in buying was so intense that five times I was asked if I wanted to sell a set of horse stirrups which I had just bought. And anything like an old television set would have several hands inside it, pulling out valves, switches or whatever. Foreigners were forbidden to sell anything in the market. They were also forbidden to take photographs of it, because it was not regarded as showing Mongolia in a good light. This was a great shame, because, with Mongolians coming from far afield with their various items for sale, the whole scene was as colourful and fascinating as one could imagine. The other notable feature was the quiet. Mongolians are usually quiet people anyway, and their tendency to enounce some words like '*ti*' (yes), by breathing in through the mouth as they speak, produces almost a whisper. It was a strange sensation to be among a crowd of thousands with no single voice raised and with the noise of shuffling feet and eager hands predominating.

For the authorities, the most presentable part of Ulan Bator is the vast square in front of the main government and parliament building. The parliament is known as the Great People's Hural, but although the Kuriltai Councils of Genghis Khan's days reflected a Mongol tradition of consultation, the Hural, under Communist rule, had deteriorated into a rubber-stamp operation once or twice a year.

Immediately in front of the starkly impressive parliament building is a mausoleum containing the remains of the national hero, Sukhe Bator, and Choybalsan, Mongolia's little Stalin. It may not be long before Choybalsan's remains are removed elsewhere (and the town named after him is renamed). But the statue of Sukhe Bator on horseback in the centre of the square will surely remain the striking sight that it is against the smooth folds of the hills in the background.

At one side of the square is the State Opera House and the recently built

Cultural Centre, its gold roof glinting in the bright sunshine. Ballet performances in the former were often very good, leading dancers having been trained in the Bolshoi Ballet. I also enjoyed (although not everyone would) the Mongolian folk singing in the Cultural Centre. Singing is very important to the Mongolians, and the tempo their songs frequently suggests is the trotting or galloping of horses. One very curious form of singing is *humi*, whereby a singer emits sounds simultaneously from chest, throat and mouth. The result is like the sound of a dangerously overloaded high-tension power cable. Yet *humi* is regarded as a very special art form, and singers have to be specially trained from an early age to develop the curious sound from three sources. The best *humi* singers apparently come from one bank of a particular river in Arkhangai province, although I never did quite understand why this should be so.

Mongolians have also developed their own musical instruments, the most important of which is the *morinhor*, a fiddle shaped like a horse's head. According to legend, a horseman, riding through the night sky, saw the tent of a beautiful herdswoman. The first night he spent in her tent was a happy one; but before dawn, he was gone. The second night he returned, to the herdswoman's delight; but again, before dawn, he rode off into the sky. After several nights of nocturnal delight yet predawn departure, the herdswoman was determined to keep the horseman with her. One night, while he slept, she left the tent to examine his horse. She noticed that the horse had little wings above its hooves. She promptly cut off the wings. When, before dawn, the horseman once again rode off into the sky, his horse crashed to earth and died. Grieving over the loss of his horse, the rider fashioned a piece of wood into a string instrument in the shape of a horse's head – and this, so the legend has it, was the origin of the *morinhor*.

Circus developed very much as an art form in the former socialist countries, and the Mongolian State Circus was well worth visiting, if only for the incredibly lithe, elastic and very attractive Mongolian contortionists. The National Museum had many interesting exhibits, particularly the dinosaur skeletons, and a nearby museum dedicated mainly to religious art had superb examples of Mongol Zurag appliqué wall hangings and striking Tsam religious masks. There was also an interesting collection of old steam and diesel locomotives at the roadside near the main station. But one museum I never visited (because I was unwilling to shed my shoes as stipulated) was the Lenin Museum. By now, if the museum is still open, it will no doubt be in order to walk around it in heavy boots.

There were a couple of hard-currency shops where one could buy very good cashmere knitwear, leather coats, fur hats, Mongolian carpets and the like. A somewhat curious practice at the hard-currency shops was the regular offer of small change in the form of chewing gum strips. This overcame a perfectly understandable local shortage of pence, cents, pfennigs and centimes, and so on. I once tried to chew one of the many chewing gums which I had acquired in this way, but it was harder than even the little Mongolian confections which are called, rather sublimely, 'milk products' but which look like popcorn made of cement. At least it transpired that we too could pass the gum strips on as hard-currency small change. If the chewing gum was no longer tender, at least it was legal. Working out just how many sticks of gum a ballpoint pen refill would cost was another matter.

Particularly attractive items on sale were the *airakh* bowls in silver, with filigree work incorporating semi-precious stones. '*Airakh*' is the Mongolian word for koumiss, fermented mare's milk. *Airakh* is not only greatly relished by the Mongolians as a nourishing and slightly intoxicating drink, it has long had traditional significance. Under earlier Chinese and Russian influences, tea drinking spread very naturally to Mongolia. Moreover, with the Russian influence and the development of wheat production in Mongolia, the Mongolians started production of their own excellent vodka, called *arkhi* (the name by which the distilled version of fermented mare's milk had been known). Originally, however, the nomadic Mongols were dependent on their animals where forms of drink, other than water, were concerned. Milk from all the different animals was relished, but it was mare's milk which was particularly suited to the process of fermentation. Fresh mare's milk is poured into a leather bag (kept hanging invariably to the right-hand side of the door of the ger), with a starter, and the bag is then beaten. *Airakh* made this way has always been highly regarded by the Mongols as the supreme product from the animal they have historically held in particular esteem as the greatest of their treasures – the horse. Before a rider set out on a journey, *airakh* would be sprinkled to speed him safely on his way, and a rider and horse winning a gruelling race would also come in for a sprinkling as a mark of honour. Similarly, a bowl of *airakh*, offered with both hands, has been a traditional way of welcoming an honoured guest. It is hardly surprising, therefore, that *airakh* bowls are often finely crafted vessels of silver.

The main shop in Ulan Bator was the department store Delguur – which, perhaps inevitably, we called Harrods (despite the fact that we never bought much more than the odd jar of Bulgarian jam there). I did hear of a Chinese market which apparently operated from June to August, but our first search for it was utterly unsuccessful. When, with very precise directions, we searched a second time, we came across a couple of stalls in the main bus station, manned by a few people of vaguely Chinese appearance. They were selling a few bundles of herbs and chives, some Chinese cabbage and a small quantity of carrots – and that was it!

It was hardly surprising, therefore, that gardening (or more specifically

36

the growing of vegetables) was a really serious matter for all of us. Each of the embassy's four married couples had their own plot in the compound. I recall jarring my arm badly when, in early May, I attempted to drive a spade into the ground. The two-inch layer of dust covered a still frozen mass below. But three weeks later my spade sank, with the first thrust, half-way up its handle. The ground, which had in the meantime thawed out, was all dust with no binding to it. Thereafter, we gardened virtually every evening, digging, planting, watering and hoeing, and, with quite amazing speed, the first lettuces, broccoli, beetroot and carrots flourished. To keep going as long as possible, I dug a half-metre-deep trench to plant lettuce in September, covering the trench with glass panes. At night, we laid polystyrene boards over the glass with blankets of newspapers, with everything covered with polythene sheets weighted down with rocks. As a result, we were able to harvest lettuce, at minus 10°C, right up to the second week in November. But then the ground froze solid, and we had to resort to planting lettuce in flower pots which we kept indoors. The results were straggly, to say the least, but they provided that little bit of something green in the Mongolian winter. It may sound ridiculous that we often served our numerous guests with a first course of a spoonful of caviar on half a boiled egg with two tiny lambs-tongue lettuce leaves, a thin slice of tomato and a shaving of cucumber; but no guest failed to appreciate such plant-pot trimmings in the extreme of winter – and there was always plenty of vodka.

In so many other ways, self-help was very much a part of our life in Ulan Bator. The embassy staff converted an old shed into an English pub which, inevitably, was called 'The Steppe Inn'. It was very well done, with mock-Tudor beams, dartboard, horsebrasses and the like. And if there was anything strange about four married couples who had spent all day, every day, working together and then, on a Friday evening, meeting up in the Steppe Inn as if they had not seen each other for months, certainly no one showed it. Moreover, visitors, whether they were journalists, businessmen, students, tourists or diplomats and couriers, all valued the little pub almost in the middle of Asia.

Apart from the four married couples, the embassy was occupied by Benson, the embassy cat. Benson regarded himself as the only permanent resident yet, whenever a married couple finally left, Benson would go absent for days in annoyance. There were several bolt-holes in the compound which only he knew about. One day, one of the wives was taking a bath when she heard frantic meowing directly underneath the bath, and then Benson's whiskers appeared through the overflow outlet at the top of the bath. One of his bolt-holes had led him along the water pipe ducts into the panelled area around the bath. We all accepted Benson, despite his terrible breath, and it was impossible to keep him out of our receptions, which he considered he had more right to attend than anyone else. But it was interesting to observe the Mongolians' attitude towards a cat. Animals were life itself to the nomadic Mongols, providing transport, clothing, housing, food, drink and even fuel. And, although the Mongols used their animals hard, they nevertheless retained a respect and affection for them. Indeed, the horse, camel, cow or yak, goat and sheep – in that order – have historically been regarded as the Five Treasures. Then, too, there was respect for wild creatures from steppe eagles to the antelope and the ubiquitous marmots. Yet cats were shunned, almost as if they had represented some evil force.

Most of our time, taken up with work, was spent in Ulan Bator. But even in the depths of intense winter, the sun would shine brilliantly in a clear blue sky. Its light on the surrounding hilltops, snow-covered in winter yet so green in summer, beckoned constantly, and whenever we had free time it was a joy to drive out into the surrounding countryside. But we would never venture out of Ulan Bator, despite the fact that our Range Rovers and Land Rovers were sturdy and very well equipped, without letting the others know where we were going. The population of the capital is roughly half a million but, outside, Mongolia is the emptiest country in the world.

The Gandan monastery, Ulan Bator.

Lama at the Tsogchin Temple, Ulan Bator.

Herdsmen in their traditional dress in Zavhan province.

Drizzle and the forlorn Erdene Dzuu, Mongolia's first monastery, which was founded in 1596, virtually on the ruins of Karakorum.

River Tuul. The Mongolian autumn is brief, before winter takes its grip.

Remote community of Mongolian Kazakh camel herders.

Winter in the hard land of Mongolia is extreme.

The weather-beaten Turtle Rock in the Khentii hill range near Terelj.

6

The 40-kilometre Limit

Without special approval, our travel was restricted to 40 kilometres in any direction from the centre of Ulan Bator. In other circumstances such a restriction would have been irritating, but as the authorities never refused our requests to make much longer journeys – and particularly because one was dependent on their making all the logistic arrangements for such long journeys anyway – the restriction did not bother us. In any case, there was magnificent countryside within the permitted area.

The most beautiful run, and certainly our favourite, was to Terelj. South-east out of Ulan Bator, the concrete slab road ran parallel with the main railway line. In winter, concrete bus shelters that we passed would be full of cows hiding from the icy winds, but in summer the roadside would be fringed with miniature irises. Also by the roadside there was for some time the very curious sight of the stern half of a large boat. I pondered deeply about this every time I passed by, because there was no lake or river for over five hundred miles deep enough to take so large a vessel. I imagined that some Russian transport driver had gone wrong on the Siberian route to Vladivostok and had simply dumped his load on the Mongolian steppe. The half ship was such an incongruous sight in that setting, yet whenever I mentioned it to Mongolians their blank looks implied either that they had not noticed it, or that they would not recognise a whole boat, let alone merely the stern half of one, if they saw it. But I may have touched a raw nerve, because one day the boat simply disappeared. Maybe, upturned, it is now serving as a winter shelter for cattle, its propeller scarcely touched by rust in the dry Mongolian climate.

It was on that route that I would invariably scan the landscape to try to spot a trace of a golf course said to have been marked out by one of my predecessors, but the relentless winds of several seasons had taken their toll. On one occasion, we thought that we had identified the first hole area, but a Mongolian herdsman had parked his ger right on top of it – he had presumably appreciated the carefully flattened ground around it. As for the other holes, the grassland was so pock-marked with holes that there was simply no telling; and a golf ball dropping into any one of them would have produced a sudden pop up by an irate marmot. One needed to be a passionately devoted player to bother with golf in Mongolia.

On a hilltop, where we would always stop to examine recent additions to a cairn and then to add stones of our own, there was a breathtaking view down to the narrow valley of the upper River Tuul. From there we would drive down into the valley, crossing the river by a wooden bridge on which one almost expected to encounter Alec Guinness and his River Kwai team. Only our steady forward movement prevented the loose wooden bridging boards from being flung up to strike the front of our vehicle. But the further we travelled up the valley, the more like Colorado the mountain scenery became – ancient rocks weathered over the ages into shapes of such amazing symmetry and smoothness, as if some giant sculptor had been at work creating shapes of elephants, monkeys and people that one could recognise. And best of all, standing entirely on its own in a side valley, was a giant rock that could only be called (as it was) Turtle rock.

Further on, at the head of the valley, are two tourist camps which consist of two hotels and some gers. Foreign tourists visiting Ulan Bator can count on being taken to Terelj, because it is a nearby area of great scenic beauty with tourist facilities. But we who came to know the area so well, and who had reliable cross-country vehicles, would make our way over a variety of different routes up the mountain slopes and then down to some idyllic spot on the river bank. In the process, our vehicles would be tested to the extreme, traversing slopes at seemingly impossible angles, fording streams, pulling through marshes and juddering over boulders on inclines exceeding 30 per cent. Occasionally, with our winches, we were able to rescue some forlorn Mongolian from one predicament or another.

A few of us would swim in the river but, even in hot August, just a few strokes in the incredibly cold water was quite enough. Yet the bubbling, crystal-clear water, like some sparkling mineral water, was so invigorating. Others would fish for arctic char, which surpassed any trout in size and flavour. And the abundance and variety of wild flowers was bewildering – gentian, edelweiss, bright-red lillies, columbines, candytuft, anemones, azaleas, clematis, poppies and daisies intermingled with many other flowers which a botanist would be hard-pressed to name.

In the very short autumn, before the night frosts singed all growth, the warm flame colours were as bright as any I have ever seen, and when winter set in the Terelj valley acquired a totally different beauty. Ice would form on the surface of the river and would get steadily thicker. Yet the water on the bottom would flow on until it eventually ceased altogether. By December the river was a block of ice some three feet thick, below which there was a gap over the totally dried-out river bed. How fish life managed to return the following season was a mystery.

Another run south took us through Zummod, the capital of Tov, the Central province, to a valley again of great beauty. At the head of it are the ruins of the Mansjir Monastery which looked as if it had been destroyed centuries ago. I was told that it was in the late 1930s that an understanding was reached there with lamas from all over the country: very few survived!

But despite the beauty of the area around Ulan Bator, it was not long before we felt the urge to travel to distant parts of Mongolia.

7

The South Gobi

I suppose it was the very name which drew us on our first long-distance journey, to the South Gobi. In an Antonov 24 aircraft, it took about 90 minutes for us to reach the provincial capital, Dalandzadgad – but it took my driver 17 hours to cover the journey in the Range Rover. He was waiting for us when our plane touched down. As we climbed out we were hit by the 37-degree temperature but, in the dry atmosphere, it was an enveloping yet unoppressive heat.

We were received by the chairman of the town council and the district party secretary who proceeded to take us on a tour. The most impressive sight was the school with its 2000 pupils and 80 teaching staff. It was on a pattern that we were to see in many outlying areas. Mongolia is so vast that education for children from areas outside the provincial centres can only be provided by bringing such children in as boarders. Mongolia was thus the only country I had visited where boarding school was as much taken for granted as it is in Britain! For all the pain that Soviet-style Communism brought Mongolia, the provision of schooling for children in such a vast and wild country has to be acknowledged as an achievement. The level of instruction covering a full range of subjects was good, and there was provision not only for the brightest to be sent on for further education in Ulan Bator but also for a wide range of vocational training. Yet once again I was struck that, although the teaching staff were bright, they knew so very little about the outside world. They had never known anything but the Communist system, and they could not conceive of any other way of life. The brainwashing to which they had been subjected, they in turn passed on. Their only objection was one which I was to hear so often in many parts of the country. The Mongolians' adoption of the Cyrillic alphabet in 1946 had led to the dropping of the teaching of the old Mongol script (Uighur). The tragic result was that virtually no Mongolian under the age of 40, which in fact meant the vast majority of the population, could read the old Mongolian literature. Cut off from this important area of their culture, the Mongolians felt deeply aggrieved.

However, I have already mentioned that my time in Mongolia

coincided with a period of gradual change. In Ulan Bator we had at first encountered resistance to our idea of Mongolian television screening our English language teaching series. It would constitute, so I was told, too much of an unacceptable foreign influence (unacceptable, it was implied, to the Soviets). But we persevered, and our series was eventually shown on television. It proved to be an outstanding success. On those evenings when the series was screened there were apparently fewer traffic accidents, the streets of Ulan Bator would empty as people gathered round TV sets, and there were horsemen who would ride into town and tie up their horses outside a hotel so as not to miss the programme. As the series continued, people would take great pleasure in greeting us in simple English, and schoolchildren started to telephone the embassy at all hours of the day and night just to use the few words that they had picked up. The series was so successful that the authorities felt emboldened to put on their own television series to teach viewers the old Mongolian script. By the time I left Mongolia, when the pace of change was speeding up, the decision was taken to teach the Mongolian script in schools.

Meanwhile, back in the South Gobi, we spent our first night in a Mongolian ger – and what a delight it was. I have already explained that the ger is roomy and comfortable, but it was a special experience, lying in bed and seeing the stars and moonlight through the open top of the ger – and, again in the early morning, to wake to the light flooding down. Our tent was one of several in the South Gobi tourist camp. After breakfast we drove to a range of mountains at the south-west edge of the Gobi, which forms the border with China. On the way we passed a small clump of knarled and weirdly shaped trees which, apparently, were a particular Gobi variety called saxaul. These trees, which can withstand long periods of drought as well as sand and snow storms, produced an almost rock-hard wood. Too hard to be worked, saxaul wood is valued as firewood because it is slow burning yet produces more heat than other wood. It is also one of the few woods which, because of its weight, cannot float in water. For us, it was just one more example of the harsh Mongolian environment making for hardness. We drove on to the Valley of Eagles, a very narrow ravine flanked by steep rock faces. As I was to find on a subsequent visit in September, when the previous winter's ice had completely disappeared, a small stream flowed the length of the valley. But that tiny stream could not have accounted for what, on my first visit in July and despite the 36°C temperature, looked like a six-kilometre-long glacier covering the base of the valley up to a height of two or three metres. It was presumably an area into which the high winds swept the winter snows off the flat Gobi expanses, where they were trapped and turned into one vast block of ice. As it was, the hot sunshine and the cool from the ice made an unusual yet particularly pleasant combination. On a grassy slope, covered with edelweiss and with jerboas scampering around, our hosts spread a very fine Mongolian carpet near a fire in an oil drum, over which lamb was being barbecued. We were joined by the GDR Minister of Education who was on holiday. As I talked to him, I noticed the pride he took in the GDR's progress. In 1987 I had heard other GDR officials talking in the same way, as if they were relieved that the GDR was becoming a little brighter and better. There was a new-found confidence about them – but barely three years later the GDR had ceased to exist.

After lunch, we drove back to the vast flatness of the Gobi. Most of the Gobi is not completely desert, for many parts of it support scrubby vegetation. However, we made for an area of what one would call proper desert, where there were very impressive dunes. We parked at the foot of a dune which towered mightily above us, and promptly started to climb up its steep slopes. It was amazingly difficult to do so – as if we were trying to walk up a hill of marshmallow in lead-weighted boots. Moreover, with every step, the disturbed sand poured in over the ankle-tops of our boots. But finally we staggered, mainly on all fours, to the top of the dune. Its crest was as sharply defined as a knife edge, yet the length of the crest trailed a plume of fine sand, as if it were smouldering in the steady breeze. As it did so, the sighing of the sand was like some haunting melody, the sound of which still rings in my ears to recall, years later, every detail of the whole scene. From the crest of the dune we gazed down at its bulk and the sweep of neighbouring dunes. On their windward sides, the steady breeze had moulded liquid-like flowing and perfectly symmetrical ripples, as if the sands had been meticulously raked by a contemplative caretaker of some Japanese temple garden. And, although the sands told their story of decay through erosion, they somehow suggested a purity all of their own. For the first time I was able to understand why it was that the Bedouin, the Tuareg, the Gobi dwellers and others could feel such a strong attachment to the barren and daunting world of sand. Clearly it has a magic of its own.

From the dunes we drove through increasingly scrubby vegetation. As we did so, I reflected on the wonders of the Gobi with its dinosaur remains, the coal deposits in certain parts, the possibility of oil reserves – and the earthquakes which could be particularly fierce in that part of Mongolia. The country as a whole receives some very powerful quakes, which would be much more of a problem if Mongolia were not such a sparsely populated country; and who is to worry about violent tremors in the empty vastness of the Gobi? Much of this book was written in the uniquely granitic islands of the Seychelles which many millions of years ago were joined with India and Africa in the vast continent of Gondwana. Chunks broke off, the seas poured in and India was carried by tectonic plate movement to crash into Asia, pushing up the Himalayas in the process. Did that impact, which is still having an effect, account for the Gobi earthquakes, on the faultline running from Afghanistan through the Tibetan plateau?

In a remote area of the Gobi we reached a lonely camel breeder's tent. Camels in Mongolia, which has the third largest herd in the world, are the two-humped Bactrian which, unlike the single-humped dromedary, can survive the intense winter conditions. Fine camel-hair is one of Mongolia's special exports, but in July the camels we inspected had been shorn, and their humps, between which we sat to ride, were quite floppy. In the breeder's tent we were offered bowls of rather salty camel's milk as well as various confections made from the milk. Milking a camel has to be a very special skill and although Bactrian camels are hardy, they take a good deal of tending. In particular, the mother camels are rather lacking in the maternal instinct, and it can take a good deal of coaxing, often with the aid of a tune played on the *morinhor*, to encourage a mother to let its infant feed. During our stay with the family we distributed balloons and sweets to the children, and gave a tin of Fortnum and Mason's tea to the breeder's wife. When, a year later, we revisited their tent, our tea tin was on proud display in the ger's *khoimor* place of honour, alongside the family photos and a Buddha.

8

The Hangai Lands of Former Capitals

Two of Mongolia's eighteen *aimags* or provinces, to the west of Ulan Bator, have similar names – Arhangai and Övörhangai – both sharing as they do slopes of the Hangai mountain range. In a number of other respects they are similar. However, it is with regard to Mongolia's former capitals that they are of particular interest.

Originally, the Mongol tribes were too small and dispersed to need a capital. Rivers, particularly the Orhon, the Selenge and, to the east, the Kerulen and the Onon, were far more significant – not that the Mongols felt themselves restricted in any way to the valleys of rivers. With their nomadic way of life, the Mongols were not settlers and builders. Within a tribe, it was enough to know who the chief was and which was his tent. Even when Genghis Khan united the Mongol tribes and led them in one conquest after another, no immediate need was felt to establish a capital. When Genghis Khan died in 1227 and Ogadei succeeded his father, the Mongols were at the height of their power. With the resources from the vast and still increasing Mongol conquests, Ogadei built a capital at Karakorum (from *kharkhorin*, meaning black sand) in what is today Övörhangai province. In its day, Karakorum must have reflected much of the wealth and ideas flowing back from the then expanding Mongol empire. But that empire's decline came quickly and, in 1388, a century and a half after it had been built, Karakorum was destroyed by the Ming invaders after the fall of Kublai's Yuan dynasty in China.

It was on the ruins of Karakorum that, a century later, Mongolia's first Buddhist monastery, Erdene Dzuu, was built (the Western Dzuu being Tibetan Lhasa itself). In a way, it is perhaps strange that Mongolia's first monastery was built there rather than at Blue Lake, where the Dalai Lama had first been acclaimed by the Mongols, or at Hovd or Uliastay, both of which were centres on the northern spur of the Silk Road. But Mongolia's first monastery having been built immediately adjacent to the site of its former capital, it seems even stranger that, barely forty years later, Mongolia's capital became the tented camp of Zanabazar, some considerable distance away, yet still within the Hangai region, at White

46

Lake (Tsagaan Nuur). The explanation is surely that, with the spread of Buddhism, Mongolia had changed to a theocracy. The search for the Incarnate resulted in the finding and identifying of the six-year-old Zanabazar at White Lake. But this does not explain why, when his tented residence-camp capital set off on its 140-year-long journey, it headed in the direction, or at least ended up at the site, of what is today Ulan Bator – instead of making, as one might have expected, for Erdene Dzuu, Mongolia's first monastery and the site of its first capital. At the time, Mongolia was under Manchu control and Mongolian secular power was in any case very limited. The residence-camp was free to wander; and maybe it did just that. Or it may have aimed at getting as far away as possible from the Manchu centre at Uliastay. Or could there have been some magnetic pull of that axis running north-east from the River Orhon towards the region of Genghis Khan's birth in today's Hentiy province?

These and many other questions were in my mind when we visited Övörhangai province, but at that time few Mongolians were able to provide answers about their pre-revolution history. Over six decades of indoctrination had had their effect, and invariably I was asked why it was that Westerners showed such interest in so evil a man as Genghis Khan.

We flew to Khujirt where there is a large ger camp for foreign tourists, and decided, very reluctantly, that there was no time in what was left of our first day to drive to the Khukhreh Falls on the River Orhon. There was not very much of Khujirt to see, even though it is a spa town with a sanatorium, so we therefore headed for the surrounding hills. On one hilltop we were struck by a virtual cloud of mountain crows, all cawing in agitation. It never occurred to us that they knew something that we humans had not sensed.

The following morning the sun shone brightly – too brightly, as we later realised. Soon after we set out, we drove through a herd of yak which straddled the rough track. Again, the animals were excited, and some of them were charging each other. Further on, goats scattered before us, fleeing in all directions – and then the first drops of rain fell. By the time we reached Erdene Dzuu the mist shrouding the surrounding hilltops was steadily rolling down the slopes towards us. The weather was set to put on a dramatic performance, heightening a feeling of desolation and, in that place with the vast yet discarded monastery standing over the vanished city of Karakorum, a sense of *sic transit gloria mundi*.

Mongolia's first monastery, which has long functioned only as a museum, comprises a large grassy area, some 400 metres square, bounded by a high stone wall. Apart from the large and ornate entrance gate, the wall has 108 gold-topped stupas set into it at regular intervals. After passing through the entrance, I noticed a weathered stone which still bore the clear engraving of the *soyombo*. The *soyombo* is a complex design, the

47

various features of which denote man and woman, continuity, life, the state, and rights and responsibilities within it. It is the Mongols' emblem, and the Communist regime retained it on Mongolia's flag (albeit topped with their inevitable five-pointed star). We also noticed some curious wooden structures which looked like road barriers. We were told that they had been presented to the Mongols by the Manchu as tokens of the preservation of order.

On the inside of the surrounding walls, pagoda-like temples and stupas were dotted around the open grassy area, and in one corner was a substantial residence which had been built for the Dalai Lama. (However, in 1904, when the then Dalai Lama sought refuge in Mongolia from the British expedition in Tibet against tsarist Russia, he resided at Urga.)

Although some renovation was being carried out near the main entrance, most of the temples looked dilapidated, with grass tufts sprouting between the roof tiles. But although the interior of the temples looked dusty, in their gloom Buddhas made of gold shone brightly. It was astounding that such priceless treasures had not only survived, but appeared to be completely unguarded – as if it were either unthinkable that they might be stolen, or that they were so irrelevant that it did not matter.

With the change which has since occurred in Mongolia, Erdene Dzuu Monastery will almost certainly be valued and restored as a major tourist attraction, and it may well once again function as a religious centre. But when I saw it, it was an awe-inspiring yet forlorn sight. In a steady drizzle we made our way out of the monastery, and across about a kilometre of open grassland to a stone tortoise – virtually all that remains of the Mongols' first capital, Karakorum. The Mongols had neither the civilisation nor the culture to leave behind the sort of riches and the richness that the world inherited from the Ancient Greeks and Romans. Nevertheless, it is bewildering that one of the largest and mightiest empires the world has ever seen left so very little trace, all the more so when its height was in the relatively recent thirteenth century.

As we drove away the drizzle turned to a downpour. We did not therefore get out of our vehicle when we were taken to see a rock on a hillside above the monastery. Ringed by a wooden fence, the rock was shaped at either end like the male and female organs. These were no casual shapes wrought haphazardly by the elements over time – we were told that erring lamas were sent to the rock to remind them of their celibacy obligations. This explanation was difficult to accept, the shapes being so realistic as to constitute an encouragement rather than a reprimand.

The rainstorm had set in as we started our journey back to Khujirt, and when our vehicle was not fording flash-streams it was dragging through deep mud. On a hilltop we saw what looked like statues of a row of camels, one behind the other. Sitting out the storm in seemingly total immobility, the camels betrayed that they were real only by the occasional flicker of a disdaining eyelid. On our return to Khujirt, we heard that a search-party had gone out to rescue a group of Polish tourists overdue from a fishing trip at the Khukhreh Falls.

Throughout that night and the next day, the rain poured down. Our return flight was cancelled and, stranded as we were in a waterlogged camp, our spirits lifted only when, in one corner, we came across a disused railway carriage (the nearest railway being several hundred kilometres away). Inside the carriage was a tourist shop – for hard currency only. As we were the only visitors with hard currency, the Mongolian attendant was delighted at long last to serve someone. It was a weird sensation, in such circumstances and surroundings, to buy cans of Loewenbrau beer and Quality Street chocolates and toffees.

The following day the rain finally stopped, but the grass runway on the steppe was too waterlogged to take the weight of an aircraft. After our over-stay of thirty hours, a Mongolian army helicopter finally came in to pick us up. A sizeable proportion of Khujirt's population seemed determined to fly with us. Somehow, the helicopter – which had a load capacity of 24 people – managed to lift off with 31 people aboard, plus suitcases, crates and barrels of fermented mare's milk. In the helicopter's stripped-down interior there was hardly room to bat an eyelid, but the door of the pilot's cabin opened a fraction and a hand passed out a note. This was transferred from passenger to passenger until it reached me. I opened the note and read, 'Dear Sir. I hope you are having a nice flight.' The pilot was one of those who had attended a short course in English given by our British Council lecturer. There was also a Mongolian mother who, uncomplainingly, was nevertheless finding it difficult to clutch her two children and all her luggage. My wife motioned that she would hold the little girl. There was something very Mongolian about the trusting way in which the child settled in my wife's arms; I spent the rest of the flight propping up the pretty head of the child who had promptly fallen asleep.

At Ulan Bator's Buyant Ukha Airport, we landed alongside another helicopter. From this, a party of serious fishermen from Austria were unloading their River Orhon catch of fish, a very substantial one despite the storm – or, perhaps, because of it.

9

Hövsgöl, the Pristine Beauty

Hövsgöl may not count as one of the wonders of the world, but in my opinion it should do.

It took over an hour by plane from Ulan Bator to the provincial centre, Mörön, and from there it was a three-hour journey over rough terrain to reach our destination. As we travelled, we advanced not only further into autumn but, eventually, into the beginning of winter itself. Although the ground surface had not yet frozen, we had entered the permafrost of the taiga region which extends northwards into Siberia. Had we dug down two metres, we would have struck the frost that never melts. Herds of horses, yaks and cows scattered as we passed on over the rough ground. Hardest of all was the manoeuvring of the Russian GAZ cross-country vehicle over the very large boulders of wide but dried-out rivers. It was a journey which would nearly have finished a person with a weak back, and it was a relief when, finally, we drove into the *somon* or little settlement, Hatgal, that was our destination. And beyond it, the shining lake Hövsgöl that I had come to see.

Lake Hövsgöl (which shares its name with the surrounding province of Mongolia) is about 140 kilometres long and 50 kilometres wide. There are numerous lakes elsewhere in the world with a larger surface area; indeed, Mongolia's salt Lake Uvs covers a larger area. But the distinction of Hövsgöl is its 260-metre depth; as a consequence the lake holds the third-largest quantity of fresh water in the world. Moreover, being in an area of permafrost, the temperatures at the bottom of the lake are so low that life forms cannot be supported in its extreme depth. This results in the water being crystal clear from top to bottom. Yet in the upper levels of the lake there is abundant fish life. With only a couple or so tiny settlements on its extensive shores, and set in a particularly remote area – even by Mongolian standards – Hövsgöl, with its surrounding forests and mountains, is absolutely breathtaking in its pristine beauty. Indeed, it was one of the most striking sights that I had ever seen, and it had a profound effect on me. It was melancholic, yet eternal and somehow secret. I gazed up at the majestic mountain, Tsagaan Uul, the white one, and I was fascinated, as I watched the snow falling on it, by the thought that waters from one slope would be swept north to the Arctic while waters from the other slope would be carried into Lake Baikal and on, maybe, via the River Amur to the Sea of Japan. The White Mountain was apparently rich in phosphates but, as I took in the whole scene, I fully appreciated what a crime it would have been had not an outcry thwarted the plans to mine those reserves. The outcry was particularly significant in that it was the first time people had spoken out against a diktat – arguably, the first time since they foiled the first collectivisation in 1932.

We went down to the settlement jetty to board the one steamer on the lake. The captain, one of three Mongolians holding a sea-going master's ticket (which was a little unusual in itself), had kindly agreed to take me for a short cruise. His ship was a very substantial one; how on earth, I asked, had they managed to get such a large vessel into landlocked Mongolia and then up to a very remote lake at over 1500 metres above sea level. It transpired that the vessel had been brought, piece by piece, from the Soviet Union over a three-year period. As we set out in this large steamer across the enormous lake, it occurred to me that it was just about the very last sight one would have expected to see in Mongolia. Our bow wave trailed back, sweeping the shoreline as if it were a shadow we were casting, which was moving with us. The red rocks on the shoreline stood out against the deep blue of the water. Beyond, little grassy clearings in the golden larch forests were dotted with pairs of Mongolian gers like tiny mushrooms. In one area there were some reindeer and the curious wigwam of a reindeer herdsman, the first that I had ever seen. In this area of Mongolia the Khalkh Mongols, who predominate elsewhere, were in a minority, the population mainly consisting of Buriats, Tsaatang and other northern tribes. On the ship's radio, there came an announcement that a snow storm was imminent; the helmsman spun the wheel, and we headed back to the little settlement.

It was evening when we docked, but I was determined to make the most of the remaining daylight. I walked through a marshy field to the patchy fringe of reeds at the edge of the lake. The water reflected shades of purple, pink, blue and grey that were entirely new to me; but then, never before had I seen the storm threat of a cold Siberian sky. As the first snowflakes started to fall I turned and made my way, through a herd of suspicious yak, to the rest-house. Inside, the lady asked me what I would like for supper. When I asked for fish, she said that she was very sorry, she only had (the usual) mutton stew – Mongolians hardly ever eat fish. And the following morning, when in response to her question as to what I would like for breakfast, I said, an egg – she again said she was sorry that there was only mutton stew. After my very early breakfast, I stepped outside as it was getting light. A metre-high band of thick mist covered the ground, from which the white-domed topped tents of the settlement protruded, their chimney-pipes carrying thin wisps of wood smoke into the still air. The waters of the vast lake steamed like an enormous hot bath. We drove up the side of a mountain to get a higher view over the lake. As we did so, bright sunshine broke out through the clouds, the mists rapidly evaporated, and the scene was transformed. The sun shone brightly in a deep-blue sky, the fresh snow on the mountain-tops sparkled, the gold of the larches was so intense one almost expected them to catch fire the very next minute, and as far as the eye could see the very special blue of the deep waters of Lake Hövsgöl. It was all a sight which burned itself on the memory and touched something deep down. Hövsgöl: the unknown, pristine beauty.

As we traced our long and rough route back to the provincial capital we followed the course of the River Egiyn which flowed from the southernmost point of Lake Hövsgöl, carrying its pure waters down to the main Selenge river which, over a thousand metres lower, eventually fed into Lake Baikal in the Soviet Union.

When we reached Mörön, the capital of Hövsgöl province, I was surprised by a number of examples of enterprise and self-help. The power station to which I was taken was using surplus heat to maintain greenhouses in which vegetables were grown. This may sound straightforward, but in a country where vegetables were not very popular – and were in any case difficult to grow – such a venture was unusual to say the least. In the light of my experience of growing vegetables in the embassy garden, I was able to have quite a professional conversation with the power station people as to the merits of various vegetables in the Mongolian climate. It was also interesting that the power station people were exploiting the new political climate by marketing their produce locally for their joint profit. This may not sound much, but at the time it showed quite remarkable spirit. Then, the town museum was of a much higher standard than any I had seen in other provincial centres, conveying a clear impression of those characteristics which were distinctive of the Hövsgöl region. The sight of a zoo, the only one in Mongolia, was certainly a surprise, the animals and birds on display again being those of the region, from reindeer to Siberian fox.

But the biggest surprise came during my meeting with the president of the town council. He listened with great patience and politeness as I chopped and changed between Russian and Mongolian. To this day, I cannot think what it was about him that made me say, 'You speak English, don't you?' His face lit up, he nodded and then started speaking very distinctly in slightly odd but beautiful English, which he had learnt in virtually total isolation. I am quite sure that, if I had not asked him, he would never have let on. For him, it would have been impolite to cut in on my mixture of Russian and Mongolian, and he would have let me leave without pointing out that he spoke English – even though this was the first chance he had ever had to speak with a native English speaker. He told me he had taught himself from every possible written and radio source. Moreover, he had established a language laboratory, which he proceeded to show me, where English, French and Japanese were taught. 'But', he said, 'English comes first.' Although there were a couple of old tape recorders, all the teaching material was home-made. It was astounding and tremendously inspiring to see such enterprise and self-help in a place which was remote from Ulan Bator, let alone the outside world.

Little wonder that my visit to Hövsgöl Province and its capital of Mörön made such an impression on me. A final surprise was that my return to Ulan Bator by air depended on the local control tower contacting a passing aircraft about landing to collect me and other passengers. But this, too, gave me a new insight.

Although Mongolia is on a spur of the trans-Siberian railway to Beijing, most of the country is distant from rail facilities. Such areas depend on overland motor transport and on air links. Air links to areas ranging from the north-west and to the south-west pass over Mörön. Because it forms such a hub for air transport and because it is situated in a broad, flat valley, there is a plan to build an airport, comparable to Ulan Bator's, at Mörön. If this is implemented, the Hövsgöl region would be opened up and the enterprising spirit which so struck me in Mörön would have a chance to flourish.

On my return to Ulan Bator, I gathered together some English language books, dictionaries and magazines which I dispatched to the president of the Mörön town council for his language laboratory. Shortly afterwards, I received a delightful letter from him, thanking me for the books. His letter continued, 'Now in our town, the weather is like the autumn one, so the livestock, the cattle breeders both feel very well. We are living now, wonderful time, dear Mr. More interesting is the reading of newspaper, watching TV – glasnost, democracy, perestroika etc'.

I never discovered how it came about that the quotation from his letter to me was published in the *Independent* newspaper in London.

10

Darhan, City on the Steppes

Darhan, Mongolia's second city, was 27 years old when I visited it in 1988. The journey to it was quite the easiest that I made outside Ulan Bator. A surfaced road has been built between the two cities. With the occasional crossed knife and fork international sign denoting a wayside restaurant, the two-hour drive seemed a remarkably normal one – only the occasional herd of goats, sheep or cows straddling the road served as a reminder that one was still in Mongolia.

Just before we reached our destination there was a turn-off to the left, marked Erdenet. This is a town, at the foot of the Mountain of Treasures, that has developed around an extensive copper and molybdenum mining complex. Off the road leading to Erdenet is a rough track to the *somon* or village of Buran-Buren, and nearby the Temple of Peace and Joy. This temple is the ancient Amarbayasgalant Monastery, and it was being restored at the time, with UNESCO assistance, by Vietnamese and Mongolian craftsmen. When the work is complete, an additional and very striking sight will be opened up to visitors – possibly on day excursions from Ulan Bator.

Darhan is some eighty kilometres south of the border with the Soviet Union. There had long been a small settlement by that name. However, after the linking of Ulan Bator to the Trans-Siberian railway in 1949, the decision was taken, sensibly, to build a new town to provide economic development in the north. Darhan was therefore built literally on the steppes. When we booked into our hotel on the edge of the city we found that, indeed, the grasslands stopped on one side of the hotel. Although it was not a lavish establishment, it was more of a hotel than any of the rest-houses that we had stayed at in other provincial centres. After we had booked in, we drove through the very tidy streets, flanked with grass verges and trees in front of apartment blocks. Although these blocks were constructed of the usual precast concrete slabs, they were not as high as those in Ulan Bator and they therefore seemed less oppressive. Moreover, each apartment's balcony had been fitted with a railing and an overhang bearing a flowing Mongolian design which, again, softened the overall block-feeling. As we drove along, pedestrians craned their necks at the highly unusual sight of a Range Rover with the Union Jack fluttering. Word very quickly got round that we were in town, to the benefit of attendance at a photo exhibition on Britain that we were to stage that night.

Accordingly, our first call was on the president of the Darhan city council. At a very modern and pleasant cultural centre he showed us where we could put up our exhibition. However, we decided to leave the assembly work until early evening, so that we could spend the day learning about the city. The president of the council gave us a briefing, and then sent an escort with us around the places of interest. We visited the leather goods factory, but the smells of the fleece-washing and leather-tanning was so bad that we did not linger. Thereafter, however, the processing became increasingly interesting. German dyes were used and Swiss designs were closely followed for end products for the Swiss and German markets; and the sheepskin fleece-lined coats, fashionable unlined Nappa jackets and skirts, as well as hats and gloves and so forth would all have found a ready market in Western countries. For our benefit, some very beautiful Mongolian girls put on an impromptu fashion show – Mongolia is not all Gobi and fermented mare's milk.

Thereafter, we were taken to a newly built and distinctly clinical palace of weddings where couples could have either a quickie or something more elaborate to seal their union in a socialist legal way. When invited to sign the visitors book, I asked for an assurance that I would not somehow be committing bigamy.

We then drove to a nearby state farm. However, despite the arrangements made before our departure from Ulan Bator to be shown around, we arrived to such a cold reception that we were not even admitted. This was the only time in my two years in Mongolia that I received the cold shoulder. I could not help recalling that, when I had paid my first call on the Minister for Agriculture in Ulan Bator and had asked him which state farms he recommended that I should visit, he referred me to the Protocol people. I replied that I would of course make arrangements for any visits through Protocol, but I came back to the point that it would be so useful to know which farms he thought it would be particularly worthwhile for me to visit. The Minister merely repeated, 'Ask Protocol.' I am sure that two years later, when it was realised that openness was here to stay, he would have been much more forthcoming, but for me that would have been too late. So it was that I stood at the very edge of the state farm's fields, just outside Darhan, and wondered what on earth could it be about agriculture that made Mongolian officialdom so secretive.

As for the earth itself, it was of a loamy blackness that I had seen nowhere else in Mongolia, and it must have been very productive. It also seemed to me, when I went round the food shops and other stores in Darhan, that the inhabitants were more fortunately placed with regard to supplies than their counterparts in Ulan Bator. The population was nowhere near the half million of the capital, yet they had access to a wide range of local produce and products. This, combined with the clean and tidy feel of the new town, conveyed an impression of a higher standard of living than anywhere else in the country. Yet in this setting above all others in Mongolia, one matter struck me as very strange. The central government had by then started to encourage private co-operative ventures, and in Darhan, Mongolia's second city, I asked to see one of these ventures. The city official looked sheepish and said, of course, he knew about the new line – and, indeed, it was an excellent idea – but Darhan had not quite got around to it; although he was sure that if I returned in a year's time there could well be a private co-operative for me to see. This, in the country's most modern city with above-average facilities, contrasted badly with the inspiring enterprise that I had seen at Mörön in the more remote province of Hövsgöl.

Culturally, of course, Darhan did not have the full range of Ulan Bator's facilities. It was hardly surprising, therefore, that, after we had assembled our photo display on Britain, a large crowd turned out for our one-night show. We had taken several bottles of Scotch with us, as well as curry puffs and sausage rolls and the like. It was touching to see the intense interest with which each and every photo was studied, as if some new planet were being glimpsed for the very first time. And, although Scotch was found to have rather a different taste from fermented mare's milk, the many exhortations that we should come more often implied that it had reached the right parts.

It was hot when we drove back to Ulan Bator the following day. We stopped twice on the way. On a hilltop, a large herd of horses had crowded together in a tight bunch. It was a weird experience, when I climbed up the hill, to watch them. One would have thought that by crowding so tightly together they would only have increased their body heat. But in the full and hot sun, there being no shade available on the hill, it seemed to me that the horses were trying to benefit from their own shade as a tight group. Every tail was swishing to keep off flies, and all the horses's flanks were shiny with perspiration. The odd hoof would stamp sharply, and whinnying from one horse would be taken up by another. It was almost like some tightly packed meeting and, somehow, I sensed that I was out of place.

Further on we stopped, literally in wonder, at the intense blue of a shallow lake reflecting the lighter blue of the sky. The grass around the lake was the brightest of greens, and was marked with the hoof prints of deer. On sand spits on the lake, plover rested in the warm sun, and on the far shore the inevitable white mushroom dots of gers. It was a moment of tranquil beauty.

11

Western Mongolia

A British scientist wrote to ask me if I could tell him about *Rhamnoides* in Mongolia. He gave no further details, and an ambassador could reasonably have excused himself for not knowing anything about *Rhamnoides*. It just happened that, as a result of my first visit to Western Mongolia, I knew quite by chance what the scientist was enquiring about. I sent him what I thought was a very informative reply, coloured as it was by my impressions of that first visit to Western Mongolia. I did not hear from him again until three years later, however, by which time I was serving in the Seychelles. I therefore had to pass the scientist's second letter to my successor in Ulan Bator for him to continue the saga of *Rhamnoides*. I can well understand it if he was not exactly enchanted by the idea.

Western Mongolia, which today consists of the five *aimags* or provinces of Uvs, Bayan O'lgiy, Hovd, Gobi Altai and Dzavhan, was a vast region which, historically, was separate from Outer Mongolia – to some extent as Inner Mongolia was. But whereas Western Mongolia joined up with the other parts of what had been Outer Mongolia on the establishment of the Mongolian People's Republic in 1924, Inner Mongolia (as well as Xinjiang, populated by Uighurs, Kazakhs and others, and later Tibet itself) was absorbed as an autonomous region of China.

My first visit was a tour for ambassadors to Uliastay, now the provincial capital of the Dzavhan *aimag*. My initial impression was one of disappointment. Uliastay and Hovd had been old centres on a northern spur of the Silk Road, along which trade had flowed in both directions. Moreover, Uliastay had been the centre of the former Manchu administration in Outer Mongolia. Maybe it was wrong to have expected to see some traces of that age and to have gained some on-the-spot insight. After all, the city of Karakorum itself had virtually disappeared without trace. Or was it that, in the short time available, we did not cover the ground sufficiently? As it was, my impression of Uliastay was that it was much like any other provincial capital. However, in a province which, at Tosontsengel, has the coldest climate in Mongolia, dropping at times to

58

minus 65°C, the golden sunny days of late June in the surrounding country were bliss. Presumably because the nights were still cold, the camels we saw when we visited a *negdel* (collective) had not yet been shorn. With the richer pasturing yet the more mountainous conditions, the camels were in any case different from those I had seen in the Gobi. The Dzavhan camels had the thickest deep-russet-coloured wool, and they were certainly the most magnificent Bactrian camels I had ever seen. The *negdel* collective, complete with its own school, hospital, shops and cultural centre, was like a large village, and it provided an insight into the way of communal life of people in outlying areas.

We drove across the grasslands, through vast herds of camels and horses roaming freely, to see herdsmen at work. One of the herdsmen asked me how many different paces horses in Britain could perform. I replied that I was no horseman, but that I thought our horses walked, trotted, cantered and galloped – so, four different paces. The herdsman smiled and said that Mongolian horses could produce eight different paces. Having spent six years in Hungary, I had seen some superb horseriding: I still recall Major Szegedi who, standing astride the backs of two horses, with three horses in front of them and five more in the front row, could drive all ten horses through a slalom at full gallop. However, the display which the Dzavhan herdsmen then put on for our benefit was in a class of its own. Mongolian horses are really very tough ponies, and it is their smaller size which apparently enables them to produce such a range of different steps. The one that impressed me in particular was a faster-than-canter pace with the horse taking very quick regular steps – and with the rider standing in his stirrups in such a way that his head bounced neither up nor down in the slightest degree.

Lunch was in the open beside a river. There were fairly dense thickets either side and, when I explored after lunch, I discovered that the thickets were covered with clusters of delicious-looking cadmium-yellow-coloured berries with bright-red tips. When I asked, I was told that the berries were *tchatsagan*. At dinner that night back in Uliastay, the berries turned up in the form of a delicious fruit juice, and also whole, as a dessert. When I asked, I was told that the berries were more widely known as *Rhamnoides*. It transpired that these berries were also processed and bottled as a syrup at Ulaangom in Uvs province, and that the syrup had proven healing properties for bad burns. Apparently, the Chernobyl nuclear disaster had led to a very heavy demand for the processed berries. When, years later, I related this to a Tirolean, he pointed out that *Rhamnoides* also grew on the banks of the River Inn, though not in profusion as in Mongolia. Mongolia has a very wide range of medicinal plants, but it seems that the soothing and healing properties of *Rhamnoides* are particularly effective and are now much more widely recognised – hence the British scientist's enquiry.

The second trip in Western Mongolia, again a tour for ambassadors, took us to Bayan Ölgiy, extreme in its distance from Ulan Bator, our flight taking over three hours. The province is also different from the rest of Mongolia in that, although it is part of Mongolia, its people are overwhelmingly Kazakhs. And, although religion had long been suppressed elsewhere in Mongolia, the Kazakhs – unlike the Mongols, who had been Buddhist – were Muslims. To the north-west, in the Soviet Union, is Kazakhstan; to the south-west, in the Xinjiang province of China, there are Kazakhs. But the High Altai mountains, as it were fencing Mongolia in at its westernmost point from adjoining China and the Soviet Union, had locked in a population of Kazakhs who, so it seemed, were perfectly content to be citizens of the Mongolian People's Republic. Apart from their Muslim religion so long suppressed that it had been virtually forgotten, the people of Bayan Ölgiy seemed free to pursue their Kazakh way of life. In many respects, we found this similar to the Mongolian way, but the differences, particularly in language and culture, were striking. All this, then, was a totally new experience for us.

We landed in the provincial capital, also called Bayan Ölgiy, on a bright, sunny day, and we gave no further thought to the weather as we launched into our programme. A visit to a carpet factory – the designs so different from the Mongol ones – then to the school and the district hospital. During a short walk around the town before dinner, an ornately designed clock permanently painted at 10.30, which I thought only conveyed a sense that at this spot, virtually the centre of Asia, time stood still. And the construction year 'I.IX.V.IX' on one building would surely have confused an ancient Roman.

Mongol Mongolian food is no great delight for foreigners, and at dinner I was to find that Kazakh Mongolian food was even less so. But the cultural show put on afterwards in the town theatre specially for us was quite spectacular. The dresses, designs, instruments and indeed the music itself were so very different. Where we had become accustomed to the oriental sound of the Mongols, we were introduced to the Turkic sound – the beguiling trilling of a song by a beautiful Kazakh woman rings in my head to this day.

The following morning we awoke to silently falling snow. At breakfast (which, with eggs and glasses of yoghurt and cream, was the best meal) we all started to wonder about our return flight the following day from that distant place. Nevertheless, we set about our programme for the day. Our first item was a visit to the local crèche where 3-year-old children were sitting statue-like on fine carpets. In another room, bundles of babies were asleep in cots. We had often remarked on the way Mongolian mothers bundled their babies like parcels to be sent off by post. In such a bundle, seemingly, a baby can move only its eyelids, everything else being bound down firmly.

After that visit we drove out into the country. The Kazakhs pursue particular sports on horseback which, although such sports are quite common in some Arab lands, I never saw the Mongol Mongolians playing. There was Kyz-kuar, for example, whereby horse riders have a tug of war over a sheepskin, while another game, Kuk-boar, involved a rider overtaking a female rider and kissing her – at full gallop! But most impressive were the Kazakh hunters with their eagles.

Kazakhs have traditionally hunted, on horseback, with eagles. In Arabia hunting with falcons is quite common, but the Kazakhs use the large Steppe eagles. The saddles of Kazakh hunters have a special stand to support their eagles, and the hunters wear a special thickly padded glove.

My first sight of Kazakh hunters remains one of my most striking recollections. Silver birch trees were dotted around an expanse of ground alternating between open grassy patches and thick clumps of bushes. It was autumn, and the leaves were already gold, yet everything was dusted with the fine snow that was falling. Russet-coloured camels were tearing at the remaining birch leaves. Silently from the bushes, two Kazakh hunters rode into the clearing where we were standing. In their long, trailing black coats and slanting hats, and with their fine beards and moustaches, they were tremendously impressive. On each saddle a hooded eagle was perched. When the *tomaga*, the leather hoods, were removed, both eagles stretched out their wings, each in a two-metre span. I showed particular interest in the *tomaga*, and this was to cause me some embarrassment at the end of my visit.

We all went into a Kazakh ger for lunch. The ger was more steeply raked than the Mongol counterpart, and the designs of the carpets and wall hangings were totally different. We all sat around the sides of the tent, and it was strange, as we sat there eating, to see snow falling through the open top and dropping with sizzles on to the hot stove beneath. After camels' milk and rock-hard camel cheese, the serious business of a sheep's head, per person, started; only to be followed by an enormous bowlful of braised parts of horse that were difficult to identify and which were probably best not recognised anyway. The *pièce de résistance* was horse sausage, which looked exactly like a horse's tapering tail. But the warmth of the Kazakhs' hospitality nevertheless made it a memorable feast. As we raised our glasses of vodka, we learnt the Kazakh toast, '*Din sow look sheen*,' instead of the more familiar Mongolian toast, '*Erool mendiin toloo*.' The Hungarian ambassador had joked that the latter sounded very similar to the Hungarian for, 'I know everything about it.' Thereafter, because I spoke Hungarian, this became the private toast between the two of us. However, back in our hotel, it was just our bad luck that dinner was yet another sheep's head per person.

The following day we should have returned to Ulan Bator, but the continuing snow ruled out any chance of flying. We therefore trekked off to fish in the swiftly flowing River Hovd. That night, when we were again offered more sheep's heads, we were able to fall back on and so very much enjoy the day's catch of Arctic char. The next morning, the snow having stopped and melted, the sun shone brilliantly. The vast but still pool of water that was the town's main square reflected the sharpest image of the town itself, the surrounding mountains and the blue sky. Our return flight to Ulan Bator seemed assured.

At the airport, as I went to board the Antonov 24 aircraft, a Kazakh presented me with the *tomaga* eagle hood that I had admired. At that very moment, I had absolutely nothing left to give him in return – but for a tin of Camembert cheese. What his thoughts would have been when he eventually opened the tin, I simply could not guess. And what he said if he delayed opening the tin of Camembert too long, I would rather not know.

A crossed cow-yak and the proud owner.

Young pioneers.

May day parade marchers. After the revolution in 1921, Mongolia became the Soviet Union's first and most loyal ally; and, in the process, the Mongolians adopted a totally Soviet way of life.

A Mongolian classroom.

Toughness born of a harsh environment.

Gateway on the steppe to the Mongolian capital.

Mongolian lama.

The ruins of the Mansjir Monastery, near Zummod, where many lamas were killed during the 1930s in Choybalsan's drive to obliterate Lamaism.

12

The Three Ancient Mongol Sports

One sunny day in May, as we were passing by, the then latest Western pop music was booming out from the open windows of the Technical University in Ulan Bator. Whether it was UB40 or Tina Turner, the tapes could only have come from Moscow, where many young Mongolians attended further education. Moreover, the then fashionable padded shoulders of trendily dressed young Mongolian women were yet another of the Western influences which filtered through via the Soviet Union. However, one influence which did not find its way to Mongolia – when it might have been expected to do so – was football. For some races, in particular contexts, feet can be insulting. It was the case that the Mongolians' traditional boots, with the flat sole yet with the toe curling up like the prow of a Venetian gondola, were so shaped as not to disturb the sacred ground. But setting aside any hang-ups which the Mongolians may or may not have had where so universally popular a game as football was concerned, they had in any case ancient sports of their own. That they had continued to pursue these sports was in itself a matter of particular note. Sovietisation had obliged the Mongolians to turn their backs on so much of their culture that it is remarkable that they were permitted to carry on with their traditional sports. The three sports in question, namely horse-riding, archery and wrestling, recall in many ways the skills of Genghis Khan's hordes (even if the sports predated Genghis Khan). In view of the attempts after the revolution in 1921 to suppress everything which had to do with Genghis Khan, it is surprising that these sports survived and flourished.

Although wrestling and archery are enjoyed at other times of the year, horse-riding is still very much a way of everyday life. The Naadam games in July bring the three sports together and mark the Mongolian sporting highlight. The main Naadam is held in Ulan Bator, usually on the 11–12 July, but counterpart events are held in the provinces (as well as in Inner Mongolia, in China). After the official opening of the games, the wrestling starts in the main stadium while the archery gets under way at a nearby range.

The wrestlers wear decorative pants and very short waistcoats like open jackets, as well as the boots with the curled-up toes. Before a bout, the wrestlers take off their spiked casque-like hats. The early bouts are usually over very quickly, thin and spindly competitors standing little change against powerful heavyweights. Winning is simply a matter of throwing one's opponent to the ground. However, as the competition progresses, increasingly only the most powerful survive and the bouts become longer. At all stages, the winner of a bout does an eagle dance. This consists of the winner taking long loping strides in his curly-toe boots until he reaches the flag and banner point, facing the audience. At this point, the winner stretches out his arms like wings and, in slow time, stamps his way around the flag. The wrestler who is the final winner at Naadam becomes a national hero. And wrestling is one of the comparatively few events in which Mongolians participate at the Olympic Games.

Both men and women, young and old compete at the Naadam archery championships. All turn out in decorative national costume, the women's blue or scarlet velvet *del* dresses shining in the sun. Many archers make their own bows and arrows. The arrows are blunt and are aimed not at a roundel-type target but rather at small birch-bark rings on the ground, which resemble children's bricks. The arrows have to drop down on to the target on the ground. The shooting is incredibly accurate, markers (who stand directly by the target) singing out the progress of an arrow in flight and finally lauding its closeness to the target. Even though the arrows are blunt bad injuries could still occur, yet, in all the Mongolian archery I saw, never did a marker flinch and never did he have the slightest cause to. This skill with the longbow is no marginal sport; it is something that carries on today from the Mongols' ancient way of life. This was summed up for me when I watched an elderly archer. It was the eye of a hunter that swept the grass, gauging and registering the strength and direction of the wind. His lungs swelled with a deep intake of air as he drew back the string of his bow, and with an almost imperceptible movement the arrow was released. The immediate look of satisfaction on his face was a sign that he did not have to wait to see the result of his shot. There was almost an inevitability about the flight of the arrow as, to the rising crescendo of the markers' singing, it fell fair and square on the target. That elderly archer possessed the skill of the hunter, warrior and *orton* – a courier of the days of Genghis Khan.

But for all that, it is the Mongolians' horsemanship that stands out. This is not something that would fit in at dressage or showjumping events, and Mongolians would find much too brief even the most testing flat races and steeplechases. Mongolian horsemanship is in a class of its own, summed up in something I once read to the effect that Mongol, horse and steppe were one integral notion.

Mongolian horses are really ponies. They may not look very impressive, but they have a toughness born of an extreme climate and a harsh terrain. They have to be survivors, and to this end they retain a degree of wildness. But the Mongol too is born of the same conditions, and accordingly there is a very special relationship between him and his horse. Many Mongolian children learn to ride before they can walk, and children are often involved in the breaking-in of horses. Mongolians often ride bareback, their saddles (which are nevertheless widely used) being awkwardly shaped contraptions made of wood. Stirrups, however, are solid affairs with a ring footplate. It is not uncommon to see Mongolians standing in the stirrups as they ride. At other times they sit on a horse like a bag of potatoes but, always, their control is masterly.

Mongolian horse races are over anything between 16 and 40 kilometres. At Naadam, the riders are all children aged between six and ten years. For weeks beforehand, training of horses alternates between long, hard runs and resting, and between feeding and starving, all designed to bring an animal up to peak performance for a 25-kilometre-long race across rough country. Before the race there is a complicated system of handicapping, after which the young riders mount their horses. They then follow the Race Master three times around the marshalling area. From the first circling of the area, which is at walking pace, the riders chant the *Giyn-Goo* songs. The second circling is at a trot, and the third and final at a fast trot. Then all – maybe as many as 1500 – make for the starting-point, and the race is on.

There is something very stirring in seeing, an hour or two later, a cloud of dust approaching from the distance as exhausted horses and riders nevertheless strain themselves over the final stretch, across the steppe, to the finishing post.

Naadam now has sideshows like aerobatics, parachute jumps, and motor-cycle stunts, but wrestling, archery and horse-races remain the essential elements. In a quiet way, Naadam awakens in the Mongolians a pride in their skills and way of life, and recalls the greatness of an ancient people.

13

Different Ways

Our ways must have seemed as strange to the Mongolians as theirs appeared to us. In Ulan Bator we were a tiny British community, living and working together in our embassy building. Commuting for me was half a dozen paces across the passage, above the hallway, which separated the residence from the chancery offices. The Mongolian residence staff were the best we had ever had in any country. They were directly employed by the Mongolian Foreign Ministry, but were hired out to us by the ministry for about three years before being rotated to work in other embassies or in the ministry itself. To do a tour in the British embassy was regarded by the Mongolian staff as something special. For them, private travel to the West was still out of the question yet, with our curious ways, we provided a tiny glimpse of a different world.

Looking back, it is amazing how our Mongolian staff settled to our strange ways and to a different routine. One of our maids was called Tsetsge (Flower); but there was also another Tsetsge who worked in two flats on the ground floor. We all called ours 'Upstairs Tsetsge' to distinguish her from 'Downstairs Tsetsge'. These names became so established that even the other Mongolian staff adopted them. 'Upstairs Tsetsge' was a small ball of energy, often to be seen hanging precariously on the outside walls as she polished the windows furiously. On her first week with us, even my water-colour paintbox was given a good dose of her elbow grease – all my carefully mixed shades being scrubbed away in the process. Then, before the first dinner party at which she helped, she was given careful instructions by the other, more experienced maid, Maajaa. When on the night it came to pouring the wine, Tsetsge poured a drop or two into my glass before she filled our guests' glasses. But she did not pour me any more wine. The following day I forgot to say anything, and at our next dinner party, once again, I was given merely one or two drops of wine to taste. When I asked Tsetsge to come back and fill my glass, she was so very sorry – but had understood that I only cared to drink one or two drops.

But there were times when we did weird things and our two maids took it all in their stride. The north-facing windows of our residence became so encrusted with two-centimetre-thick ice that the kitchen and bedroom became quite gloomy, despite the bright sunshine outside. When the maids saw me trying to chip the ice away, they promptly came and helped. It took three hours to clear three windows. No sooner had we finished than the windows promptly froze over again, and by evening the ice crust was as thick as ever. But if window-ice on the north side got us down, there was beauty and sheer magic to the ice which formed overnight on our south-facing windows. The bright, early morning sunshine would illuminate the most amazingly symmetrical crystal formations which would sparkle gold and silver, casting rays of the entire colour spectrum.

Every morning, Tsetsge would come in and fill all our humidifiers, each of which consumed a bucketful of water a day. I wondered how she described to her friends these strange electric machines, the purpose of which seemed to be merely to get rid of water. It would not occur to Mongolians that they lived in a particularly dry climate in which rust was virtually unknown, and that foreigners did not have their tolerance of dryness. In winter, the dryness made static electricity a great problem for us, despite the humidifiers. Not only was kissing hazardous, I broke the loudspeakers of three radios by releasing a heavy charge when I touched them suddenly. The local World Health Organisation representative said that, in Mongolia, a person could release a charge of ten thousand volts. When I looked doubtful, he explained it as one-dimensional only and therefore not lethal.

It was a tradition that, just before Christmas, our driver and the embassy handyman, Olzii, would drive off, some hundred kilometres or so, to cut a fir tree for us (the trees around Ulan Bator being mainly silver birch and larch). This was a day out which they obviously enjoyed, involving much consumption of fermented mare's milk with various friends on the way. When they returned, the bare trunk of a Christmas tree was lashed to the roof of the Land Rover with all its branches stuffed in the rear of the cab. We protested that we had wanted a proper Christmas tree with all its branches intact. Olzii was quite nonplussed: he said that that was the way he had always done it, and he assured us that we would be delighted with the result. Next day, a perfect Christmas tree stood in the embassy hall. Olzii had, as in previous years, stitched the branches back on to the trunk, the result being far more symmetrical than nature's original efforts. Later on, Olzii knocked on all our front doors. When asked what the matter was, he merely blinked his eyelids rapidly. He then pulled us all down to the hall. By using the starter device from a fluorescent light, Olzii had got the Christmas tree lights to blink – which the manufacturers had never designed them to do in the first place. Olzii, a big and powerful Mongolian who really had no idea what Christmas meant, had had all of a child's delight in decorating the tree.

I had never previously been in a country where Christmas simply did not exist. Mongolia had been reduced to a solitary functioning Buddhist monastery, and the one small Orthodox church that had been at Urga in tsarist times had long since disappeared. It was therefore very difficult for the eight of us then in the embassy to feel that it was Christmas. Matters were made worse when our Christmas mail from home – as well as the turkeys we had ordered – did not arrive. However, as happened so often for us in Mongolia, something turned up at the last minute. The Mongolian Foreign Minister sent me a superb Siberian goose which was quite large enough for all eight of us. It was the first time in my diplomatic career that I had cooked a foreign minister's goose.

I hope that it has already emerged that I acquired a very special regard for the Mongolians, but the one aspect of their way of life that was difficult to take was their food. Remarkably, in several parts of the Far East, but particularly in Hong Kong and the Philippines, Mongolian Hot Pot features regularly on menus. Even in Singapore and Malaysia, the virtually identical 'Steamboat' is a popular and very sociable form of evening meal. With the wide range of tropical vegetables and seafood available, Steamboat can be a very elaborate and satisfying meal. The Malaysian Steamboat was identical to the Hot Pot vessel, consisting of a round lower holder for glowing charcoal, with the fumes escaping upwards through a central funnel. Ringed around the funnel was a circular container for boiling water or stock, ready to receive the choice pieces for cooking at the table.

On the first occasion I tried the Hot Pot in Mongolia, it was indescribably bad. The meat stock in the ring was indeed boiling, but into it were poured cold fried potato chips plus a few other dismal vegetables. The soggy and tasteless mess put me off Hot Pot. Months later, we and other guests were entertained not only by the new but by the very first American ambassador to Mongolia, in the ornamental ger which was erected for such occasions on one of the upper floors of the Ulan Bator Hotel. (The Mongolian capital may not have boasted a hotel with a revolving restaurant, but no hotel in London, Paris or New York that I could think of had a tented restaurant!) With the view over the city it was a very striking setting, but my spirits fell when I noticed that Hot Pot was on the menu. In the event it was really very good, the meat stock being flavoursome with pieces of lamb in it and the vegetables crisp and tasty. Clearly, a Hot Pot could be good only if the ingredients were up to scratch. However, although Mongolian Hot Pot is widely known in the Far East generally, it is not a particularly common dish in Mongolia itself.

The Mongolians are passionately fond of meat, particularly mutton.

They maintain, with justification, that their mutton has the distinctive taste of the wild herbs of the steppe grasslands. Meat is eaten very often as a stew, possibly with vegetables like potatoes, onions and carrots. But the Mongolian climate, particularly in winter, is almost as far from the ideal as one can imagine where the growing and storing of vegetables is concerned; and the truth of the matter is that the Mongolians are not very keen on vegetables in any case. Neither, for that matter, do they like fish, despite the fact that the unpolluted rivers produce outstandingly good freshwater fish. But for foreigners, a diet of mutton stew can become very tedious (particularly in winter, when the smell of mutton seems to seep into clothing and buildings). For special occasions, the Mongolians delight in *buuz*. These are little squares of dough with chopped mutton and onions in the middle, the four corners of each dough square then being drawn up and crimped into a parcel-like dumpling for steaming in a cloth. *Buuz* can strike the visitor to Mongolia very much as the national dish. However, steamed dumplings are particularly distinctive and typical of the Beijing and the north-eastern area of China, and it could therefore be that the very Mongolian *buuz* in fact originated in China. *Buuz* are very acceptable – but not when they follow a main meat course, which itself followed a cold meat course!

On one occasion, I visited a little workshop in Ulan Bator to have a picture framed. In the workshop, I saw a particularly striking model of a Mongolia ger. When I asked the craftsman who had made it if he made such things for the tourist trade, he merely asked, 'Why?' I replied that more and more tourists were visiting Mongolia and that the little model ger was exactly the sort of thing they would surely like to buy. He could make more money that way. Again, the craftsman asked 'Why?' That evening I related this story to a highly intelligent Mongolian who had spent a good deal of time in Britain and the United States. He replied that he understood my point: indeed, Mongolia needed to earn as much hard currency as it could. However, I should understand that what might seem only common sense in the West was based on Western conditions and attitudes. Conditions in Mongolia were different and attitudes reflected more of a simple contentment.

Mongolia is one of the few countries in the world which is trying to increase its population. The more children a woman had, the greater the financial assistance (and the more medals) she received. With the very small size of their country's population, the Mongolians were particularly worried about the spread of AIDS – not because it was widespread, but because of the potential threat to so small a population. Where strikingly less concern was expressed was over the Mongolian diet – which was one thing for nomads, burning off energy in extreme climate conditions, but was quite another matter for the increasing number of Mongolians living in urban centres and performing sedentary office or factory work. Whether their dislike of fish and their disinterest in vegetables are to be attributed to the former ban, on religious grounds, on fishing and cultivating is by now irrelevant. The Mongolians remain predominantly meat-eaters, with mutton as the virtual staple diet. In Ulan Bator there was a short summer supply of tomatoes and cucumbers but, although potatoes were nearly always available, supplies of onions, carrots and cabbages were erratic at other times of the year. As storage in the cold winter conditions was a problem, the quality and, hence, the nutritional value of the vegetables left a lot to be desired. Perhaps strangely, the Mongolians did not go in for pickling vegetables, which is such a feature in Eastern European countries.

In early June, after the foals have been taken from their mothers, the mares are often tethered beside the gers for regular milking. The milk, as already explained, is beaten in a leather bag to produce fermented mare's milk, called *airakh*. The first of the new *airakh* apparently has a laxative effect on the drinker: as one Mongolian proudly told me, 'It cleans you right out.' But thereafter, the daily consumption of *airakh* reduces the amount of meat that a Mongolian needs to eat – and since *airakh* has a slightly intoxicating effect anyway, the whole process is regarded as one of the joys of summer. During the summer months, the cattle and sheep fatten on the lush grass, building up meat reserves for the long winter months. Some *airakh* is kept frozen for special occasions in the winter, and some of the fermented mare's milk is distilled.

In short, the Mongolian diet thickens the blood and builds up body fat as resistance against the intense cold of winter. But the urban Mongolian does not have a chance to burn off energy in the way that his counterpart out in the country does. In these circumstances, heart diseases are probably a greater threat to the Mongolians than AIDS.

For all that, the Mongolians are handsome people, and they look very striking in their national dress, the *del*. The *del* is a high-necked coat (for men) or dress (for women) which is gathered at the waist by a broad and brightly coloured sash. The *dels* for festive occasions are highly decorative, being made from silk, satin or brocade. Men's working *dels*, however, are very practical garments. With an underlayer of fleece or felt, they are warm. The centre fold over the chest provides a holder for the odds and ends that would otherwise be carried in pockets, and the excessively long and widening sleeves provide cover for ungloved hands. Many men wear trilby hats, although fur hats are also very common – invariably with the ear flaps hanging loose, almost as a sign of indifference to the biting cold. Knee-high boots are the rule, made either of leather or felt.

The faces of people in country areas are invariably weather-beaten, and the faces of the elderly are a contrast of skin drawn tightly over high cheek bones, yet deeply creased around the eyes, conveying a sense of long experience yet tranquillity. Quite often, the cheek-bone area of country people's faces is bright red and even scarred from icy wind-chill, and many people suffer eyeball lacerations from the fierce dust storms of spring. But, in summer, when Mongolian women exchange their heavy winter clothing for light floral, and often very fashionable dresses, they can be strikingly beautiful. Regular visits to the hairdresser are regarded as essential – and once again it was noticeable that hairdos were in tune with the latest fashion.

On summer evenings, with daylight until about ten thirty in the evening, people would stroll along the streets, stopping for an ice cream or for a glass of kvass, a drink made from bread. And in one part of the city or another, one could hear Western pop music as students put on their own disco events.

However, most of all, inhabitants of Ulan Bator liked to get out of the city to a small dacha in one of the many dacha colonies in surrounding areas. Special buses were laid on to carry people to and from their work in the city and, for a few short months, there was the chance to return in the evening to the rustic environment of a dacha colony. Yet even in Ulan Bator there were the permanent ger settlements similar to those in all the other parts of the country. These settlements consisted of long rows of gers and wooden huts, all surrounded by pallisades into which gates were set at regular intervals. These gates were often brightly painted and bore the symmetrical religious designs so often depicted in Mongolian art. The designs, which varied from the rounded to the angular, nevertheless all featured an unbroken line, denoting continuity, such as a diamond, extending beyond its four points to form four other diamonds linking back into the central one. But then two overlapping diamonds (or overlapping circles) often featured on Mongolian wedding rings, denoting continuity through union of man and woman. For as it is written, 'the lucky design is woven of golden threads of human feeling for friendship, signifying the common background of mankind and the endless happiness in the hearts of all.'

The Mongolians have a wide variety of indoor games and puzzles. Many of these, such as link chain puzzles, almost certainly came from China. But games and puzzles involving the bones of animals and pieces of stick are probably of Mongol origin, and some of the puzzles can be as perplexing as a Rubik cube.

One fascinating game I once saw was a group of men playing a Mongolian version of curling. But in place of the curling iron, the Mongolians used small missiles about the size of a cigarette packet. These puck-like missiles appeared to be square, but were in fact octagonal. Each player had made his own, and all the pucks I saw were beautifully crafted.

They were thrown along the smoothest ice at a marker some eighty metres distant. Thereafter, the idea was to knock opponents' pucks out of the way, the winner being the player whose puck ended up closest to the marker. If all this sounds like curling or bowls, the excellent singing and chanting which accompanied each throw and which rose to a crescendo or fell away altogether, depending on the accuracy of a throw, was quite distinctive.

Another amazing sight was to see Mongolians making felt. A large area would be covered with sheep's wool. The layer of wool would then be flattened before being dampened with water. Thereafter, the layer would be rolled up around a long pole. With this rolling finished, the two ends of the pole would then be harnessed to a horse. A rider would then spur the horse and charge off dragging the pole behind. After this rough treatment, the pole would be detached and the resulting layer of impacted wool would be unwound to dry off.

The Mongolians could demonstrate extraordinary skills where things like horse-riding and cattle rearing, which went with their way of life, were concerned. But when their interest was not engaged, they tended to stand back. On one occasion, when poles to carry cables for a new trolley bus service were being erected in a street in Ulan Bator, one pole went through the main water pipe – at minus 27°C. Water gushed out under pressure, yet froze immediately, and the main road in question was soon transformed into a frozen river. Some Mongolian workmen turned up – but it was left to Soviet specialists to cope with the problem. The conditions were appalling, especially when it got dark and the temperature plummeted. It was a new insight into the dogged determination which Russians can bring to bear. They may be lacking where matters like courteous service are concerned, but those Soviet specialists laboured hard for ten hours, without a break or any refreshment, in soaking clothes which froze on their backs. Only by using jets of steam were they able to melt the constantly forming ice, in order to replace the broken pipe and to tighten the nuts and bolts.

Yet it was amazing that the traffic still circulated on the treacherous frozen river that was the main road, without a single accident. Roads are invariably treacherous in Mongolia in winter, but it was extremely rare to see an accident caused as a result of the wintry conditions. The Mongolians take winter in their stride. No one would think of complaining about pavements which were like glass. But then virtually everyone from schoolchild to army officer in uniform, from demure office girl to old lady, would enjoy taking one or two quick steps before launching into a long slide on the pavements. Winter was fun.

14

As to Hentiy – and so on

There were many places in Mongolia that I did not manage to visit. I never made it to Hovd, which, like Uliastay, had been a centre on the northern spur of the Silk Road; nor did I visit Uvs province, bordering the ancient but subsumed land of Tannu Tuva (recalled now, mainly by the older generation of collectors, for its large triangular and diamond-shape postage stamps).

In particular, I was put out that I finally had to leave Mongolia just two months before a special trip, which the authorities were arranging, to Khalkhyn Gol, in the extreme east of the country, to mark the fiftieth anniversary of the victory there in 1939 of the joint Soviet–Mongolian forces over the Japanese. Although the Battle of Khalkhyn Gol took place before the outbreak of the Second World War, it was nevertheless the first major defeat that the Japanese suffered. The Japanese had penetrated, up through Manchuria, too far north, and their lines of communication had become overextended by the time they crossed over into the harsh terrain of Mongolia. Khalkhyn Gol was also the first of the victories of Zhukov, who commanded the Soviet–Mongolian forces; arguably, however, the imminence of the Second World War saved him. Stalin, who had purged so much of the Red Army's leadership in the 1930s, could so easily have seen Zhukov's success as one more threat. In a number of respects, to have been at Khalkhyn Gol on May 1989, when the fiftieth anniversary was marked by Mongolians, Russians and Japanese, would have been an unusual experience. But for me it was not to be.

Nevertheless, most of all, I regretted not having visited Hentiy province, a land of distinctive beauty and special interest. No one has so far traced the grave of Genghis Khan (although the search for it goes on). However, it seems likely that his grave is in Hentiy province, the land of his birth.

It may be asked, as so many Mongolians did – at least, when I first arrived in Mongolia – why I keep coming back to Genghis Khan. In fact, it was one of the most striking signs of the changing times that by the time I came to leave Mongolia, the Mongolians had not only rediscovered

Genghis Khan, they were on the way to rehabilitating him. There was talk of naming a new hotel in Ulan Bator, as well as a street, after him. That is one matter; but the Mongolians may yet overdo it by making Genghis Khan into a national hero out of proportion to the cruelty and havoc he wreaked. However, for me, it is less a matter of fascination with Genghis Khan himself than sheer amazement that, less than eight centuries ago, the Mongols – a simple people despite their toughness – conquered more of this world than anyone else before or since. Of course, his success in uniting the tribes in the first place and the will-power that launched them forth and propelled them on cannot be overlooked. It needed a Genghis Khan to ignite the Mongols. But it was a particularly distinctive toughness, born of a hard environment, that took such a simple people, progressively adding conquered resources to their strength, so very far. To see Mongolia today, when much is still unchanged by man, is to gain at least some insight.

I once visited Reykjavik on a short assignment and was struck by the depressing effect which winter had on the Icelanders. In fact, I heard it suggested that Greenland and Iceland should swop names – because, although Iceland had large glaciers like the Vatnajökull, it was not generally the icy country which outsiders might imagine it to be. The icy Arctic winds may blow down on Iceland, but they encounter the tip of the Gulf Stream, making for a very changeable and damp climate. However, immediately below the Arctic Circle as Iceland is, winter daylight is very short with some days having hardly any real daylight at all. In short, the long, dark winter must indeed be very depressing for the Icelanders and other Nordic races.

The Mongolians, in contrast, never seem depressed by their winter, even though it was much harsher. The inhabitants of Ulan Bator may have looked forward to summer, but very often this had to do with their escape from the concrete apartment blocks to a little dacha on the outskirts – or, better still, to a ger. The one thing which makes the Mongolian winter tolerable, enjoyable even, is the regular bright sunshine. Situated, like Vienna and Vancouver, on a latitude of about 48 degrees, Ulan Bator enjoys a reasonable amount of winter daylight in any case. But the country's average of 240 days a year of sunshine and bright-blue skies extends into the winter months. Even so, the Mongolian winter is not only harsh, it can be cruel in the toll it takes of man and beast. The intensity of winter, the hardness of the land, the awe-inspiring emptiness and the very absence of anything moderate could easily make for a sense of depression. Yet the Mongolians have adapted to such conditions and draw strength from them.

As with other races, contrasts characterise the Mongolians. They are still hardy and tough, yet they have a touching serenity. They are enigmatic, but respond wholeheartedly to friendliness. They can be lazy, but can be astonishing in their resourcefulness. It was the Cuban ambassador who told me that *maragash* was the Mongolian word for 'tomorrow' without, he added, the degree of urgency that *mañana* implied. Yet in the depth of winter and at a completely isolated and remote spot, I saw a woman hack blocks of ice from a frozen pond and then carry the blocks two kilometres back to the family tent (the only sign of life for as far as the eye could see). On another occasion I watched some welding in progress. However, the power cable was not long enough. As there was no other cable, the workman promptly cut the cable in two – to insert long iron poles between the cable ends. This enabled the current to flow far enough for the job to be completed. It is easy to dismiss this as foolhardiness, but that would be to misapply our standards to bleak circumstances. The fact that supermarkets in the West stock brand after brand of mineral water in large plastic bottles or in bulbous-shaped little glass ones is totally irrelevant to a woman who, to satisfy her family's need for water, has to hack ice out of a distant pond. It is in adversity that the essential value of resourcefulness shows up.

All this points to the simplicity of the Mongolians; and, indeed, they can be naïve and unworldly. But the other side of the coin is that they are in harmony with nature and draw strength from it in a way that many of us have long since forgotten. A good deal of the inner strength of the Mongol of the Genghis Khan era remains in the Mongolian of today. But for all that, the descendants of a once proud people had become cowed. Decline had taken a very heavy toll; Mongolia was wedged between two of the largest of all states, and both were overbearing. In desperation, the Mongolians sided with the Soviet Union and, in the process, had to sublimate themselves almost totally to Soviet ways.

Molotov had at one time been Soviet ambassador in Ulan Bator; although this appointment was a demotion which followed his fall from grace, his stature and attitude nevertheless underlined the point that the Soviet ambassador was a virtual viceroy in Mongolia. Every Mongolian ministry had its Soviet adviser and, apart from some seventy-five thousand Soviet servicemen in the country, the presence of about thirty thousand civilian specialists ensured that there were few areas of life in which the Soviet influence was not felt.

In 1987, although the changes under Gorbachev were beginning to challenge the whole structure of vested interests in the Soviet Union, they had by then had little effect in Mongolia. My initial call on the Foreign Minister would normally have been an occasion, on the day before I presented my credentials, for an exchange of courtesies. But I was then the only Western ambassador in Mongolia and the Foreign Minister used the occasion for a totally unnecessary and offensive harangue regarding so-called Western foot-dragging over Soviet disarmament proposals. However, in 1988, a new and younger Foreign Minister took over, who reflected more of the new thinking of the then Soviet Foreign Minister, Schevardnadze. I was invited to attend an international conference, organised by the Mongolians, to do with disarmament. Not only were my remarks, reflecting the Western position, listened to, they were reported in the Mongolian press. Moreover, when in 1988 – the year which marked the 25th anniversary of the establishment of diplomatic relations between our two countries, I asked to make an address on Mongolian television, arrangements were promptly made for me to do so; I was probably the first Western diplomat to speak on Mongolian television. It was no great event, but it was taken by many Mongolians with whom we were in touch as a sign that *glasnost* (or, as they called it, *il tod*) was spreading in Mongolia.

At that time, there was a remarkable contrast between areas where the Mongolians held to their long-instilled ways and those in which they warily tested the new freedoms.

In 1988, May Day was yet again marked in Ulan Bator with the old-style sort of parade which was no longer seen in Moscow. Moreover, loyalty having traditionally been taken seriously by the Mongols, old Mongolian veterans, proudly wearing their campaign medals, simply could not understand the dismantling in the Soviet Union of Stalin's image. Indeed, Stalin's statue in Ulan Bator continued to stand long after virtually every counterpart elsewhere had been pulled down. Hard lessons had long been learnt the hard way – and one should not change direction until one was sure.

It was over the environment that Mongolians first started to question the authorities. The government had a plan to exploit the substantial phosphate reserves in the White Mountain, immediately adjacent to the pristine Lake Hövsgöl. As previously mentioned, expressions of public concern thwarted these plans. However, it was almost certainly the case that Soviet environmentalists had been behind the Mongolian protest in the first place. There was already a strong lobby in the Soviet Union against the pollution of Lake Baikal – and waters from Lake Hövsgöl feed into Baikal! However, success in stopping the phosphate mining beside Lake Hövsgöl led the Mongolian environmentalists to take on other targets such as open-cast coal mining, the land degradation caused by the copper mines at Erdenet, and arable farming methods which led to soil erosion – even though, as in the case of the Erdenet mining complex, this led to some crossing of Soviet interests, with background murmuring about foreign exploitation of Mongolia's wealth.

Protests over environment issues came quite naturally to the Mongolians, with their inbred affinity to their natural surroundings.

Resentment, so long held in check, over suppression of their culture inevitably acted as the spur to what might be called cultural reforms. The reintroduction of the teaching of the old Mongolian script, thus reopening the old literature to the people, renewed interest in Queen Mandkhai and Genghis Khan and the restoration of the traditional White Month Lunar New Year festival were some of the first moves forward in the Mongolians' rediscovery of their culture. This was heady stuff, and there was every reason to believe that they would press steadily on in that direction.

However, with the Mongolians not having had the slightest experience of a democratic tradition that they could draw on, and because they had been imbued with the belief that politics could only be Marxism–Leninism, moves for political reform arising from within Mongolia itself could hardly be expected. It seemed likely that political reform would have to wait upon the spur of examples in other countries.

As to economic reform, the government followed virtually every move which was made in the Soviet Union in that direction – inevitably, with as little success. However, the government's efforts in one particular direction met, initially at least, with a poor response; and, in the light of what I had seen in Hungary, this surprised me. Even at the time of my first arrival in Hungary in 1968, moonlighting was common. When in succeeding years a little more private enterprise was permitted, step by step, Hungarians were only too eager to make full use of such new opportunities. In 1988, the Mongolian government, again following the trend in the Soviet Union, allowed for a modest level of private enterprise, albeit operated as workers co-operatives. In marked contrast to the Hungarians, the Mongolians showed hardly any interest in this new opportunity. A Communist government found itself in the curious position of trying to urge a little private enterprise on reluctant workers. The odd hairdressing and picture-framing venture did eventually get going, as did a disco-bar. But there was certainly not the rush that one would have expected. This said something either about the Mongolian work ethic, or about a disinterest in earning more money. The one area in which the new scope was taken up more readily was animal husbandry. People were allowed to own a larger number of animals, and this was something Mongolians could understand. It was a move (if yet too small) distinctly in the right direction for people and the state. Cattle breeding had long been a major economic activity in Mongolia. At one time, Stalin called for a Mongolian herd of two hundred million – although, after him, the target was lowered to eighty million head. But, although the Inner Mongolians in China achieved a herd of forty million, the (Outer) Mongolian herd had still to reach even a stabilising twenty-five million. Spring storms, with a lack of adequate shelter and fodder, took a heavy toll. However, Mongolians have a feel for animals – all the more so if they own them. With improved provision and transportation of fodder and the building of basic sheltering, especially for young animals, Mongolia could go on to reach its full potential as a producer of meat and other animal products – including, in particular, cashmere wool.

There were very good reasons, which have already been covered, as to why the Mongolians did not rush, as did their counterparts in Eastern Europe, to embrace the opportunities that change was opening up. The truth of the matter is that Mongolia had never really been independent. It was to take time for the Mongolians to realise that the changes sweeping through other countries were inevitably going to affect them, a people which had never before considered that it had any choice.

15

New Windows on the World

A Mongolian once asked me if I was 'Russkii?' I replied that I was 'Angliskii'. The man looked puzzled and then asked, 'Nyet Germanskii?' To make sure, I replied in Mongolian, 'Baghwee, Angoliin'. He looked utterly confused until he made up his mind and pronounced that I must be 'Angliskii Germanskii'. All this may sound like a translation of some old-time musical hall repartee. But perhaps it also said three things. Firstly, the Russian influence was so strong that the Mongolian spoke and used Russian as a matter of course. Secondly, the GDR had pushed assistance to Mongolia to the extent that it was not unreasonable to assume that a European who was not Russian could only be German. Thirdly, the idea of a person being something different, called English, was beyond grasp.

Historically, there were no links between Britain and Mongolia. With India the jewel in the crown, the Great Game and British expeditions to Afghanistan and Tibet to forestall tsarist Russian expansion were not matched by British interest to counter Russian expansion further eastwards to the north of China. In any case, Mongolia was a well and truly landlocked country which produced neither tea, spices nor porcelain. Inasmuch as there was any British concern with furs and skins, no doubt the Hudson Bay Company was adequate. In short, Mongolia was outside our sphere of interest.

The Hungarian and Mongolian languages share some two thousand roughly similar words. The Hungarian word *tenger* means the sea. Basically the same word in Mongolian means the sky or universe (hence, Genghis Khan – Lord of the Universe). My somewhat obscure point is that the landlocked Mongolians have had no feel for the sea, and their understanding of countries beyond the seas was very restricted. But then, in Britain, most references which are made, surprisingly often, to Mongolia are not to do with the country itself but rather to call to mind one extreme or another. Not even Timbuktu sounds quite as remote and extreme as Outer Mongolia.

For all that, Britain has had its fair share of Mongolists. Although

Professor Owen Lattimore (who, after being unwarrantedly caught up in the McCarthy purges of the early 1950s, settled for some time in England) is no longer alive, there are several internationally respected British academics with the same dedication and enthusiasm, guiding a new generation specialising in the field. Future prospects for the work of Mongolists are bright because a difficult subject will no longer be clouded by layer upon layer of secrecy – which formerly was not merely instinctive but was an integral part of Mongolia's authoritarian regime. Moreover, British academic interest in Mongolia has broadened into other special-ised fields, such as geology, medicinal plants, flora and fauna, camel breeding, religious tracts, yurt (that is to say, ger) history, dust storms and so on.

It was in 1963 that diplomatic relations were established between Britain and Mongolia, and the British mission in Ulan Bator was opened in 1965. That the United Kingdom had been the only Western country to open and to retain an embassy in Ulan Bator was very much appreciated by the Mongolians. We increasingly provided a tiny window for them to the world beyond China and the then Soviet bloc, particularly where the English language was concerned. The British Council maintained a particularly valuable English language teacher at the Mongolian State University who, aside from the main job of teaching teachers of English, always found time to meet *ad hoc* requests for special courses for pilots, air traffic controllers, tourist guides and hotel staff (Western tourists to Mongolia having built up to ten thousand a year by 1987). The British Council had also been sending Mongolian students to Leeds University on English language courses since 1965. If, by the time I arrived in Mongolia, every government department still had its Soviet adviser, most also had at least one member of staff who was invariably proud to announce, 'I was at Leeds.' And at our annual 'Old Leeds Boys and Girls' reunion, it was not unusual to hear Mongolians singing 'On Ilkla' Moor bah't 'at'.

The very first UK–Mongolia Round Table, which reviewed the whole range of relations and links between the two countries, was held in Ulan Bator in 1987 at precisely the time when the Mongolians felt freer to develop their relations with a Western country. It marked not only the start of a new dialogue, a major advance in itself, it set a new tone to our bilateral relations right across the board. The more relaxed format of round-table discussion was a refreshing novelty for the Mongolians, accustomed as they had become to meetings of a set-speech type. The result was a new rapport, of direct benefit to the very first British trade mission to Mongolia the following year and which in turn led to a second trade mission in 1989. Our two markets were too distant from each other, particularly given Mongolia's deeply landlocked situation, for bilateral trade to be very great. But the trade missions put our commercial relations on a firm footing and, in the meantime, there have been quite significant commercial developments – such as a British company opening up Mongolia's communications with the outside world.

Another new window was provided when, in 1988, the Americans began to open their new embassy. For the Cubans, the Mongolian winter was an unmitigated penance, while our Indian neighbours were in just about the last place on earth for the vegetarians that most of them were. But the cheerfulness and resilience with which the first American diplomats set about establishing their mission was striking. Mongolian meeting American was as much the meeting of two different worlds as it was possible to imagine. On a trip to Western Mongolia, an American diplomat tried to buy a camel saddle with US dollars. The Mongolian owner of the saddle looked very sceptical about such a transaction, maintaining that tugriks were real money. The following day, as the diplomat was about to board his return aircraft, the Mongolian rushed up to say that he had been talking to his friends and they had said that those dollar things were not too bad, so maybe they could do business after all. Yet when the US Senator for California visited a cattle-breeder's tent outside Ulan Bator, the Mongolians arranged for a party of American tourists, who just happened to be from California, to visit the same cattle breeder at the same time. This occasioned comments from the tourists that, never having met their senator back home in California, it was the very last thing they expected to come face to face with him in a cattle-breeder's tent in Outer Mongolia.

The Japanese had long maintained an embassy in Ulan Bator, staffed with a number of good Mongolian-speakers, but the Mongolians were not inclined to get ahead of the Soviet Union in developing relations with Japan. Japanese war widows were permitted to visit the war graves at Khalkhyn Gol, and, for their part, the Japanese provided valuable assistance over Mongolian commercial and cultural exhibitions in Japan. Nevertheless, Mongolian–Japanese relations seemed to be in suspended animation, awaiting their time to move forward.

Until the opening up which came with the Gorbachev era, the only relations that mattered to the Mongolians were those with the Soviet Union and other Communist countries. Apart from academics' interest in Mongolia, there had been no links between Mongolia and the United Kingdom until diplomatic relations were established in 1963. Our mission in Ulan Bator opened in difficult times of continuing East–West tension, but we were the only Western country to keep at it. In the process, a range of links were established, particularly with regard to the English language. When Mongolia eventually started to look beyond its previous horizons, the relationship with Britain came into its own. Something which, alongside Mongolia's preoccupation with Marxism–Leninism, had been marginal was already in place when the post-Marxism–Leninism period came for Mongolia to look to its own future. The marginal became directly relevant: relevant in itself, and as a signpost to the broadening of Mongolia's relations with other Western countries and organisations like the European Community, the Asian Development Bank and the International Monetary Fund.

Erecting a Ger-tent frame.

A Mongolian Ger-tent.

Inside a Ger-tent.

Mongolia's short autumn.

Steppe in summer.

Mongolian curling.

Bayan Olgii.

Mongolian Kazakh hunter.

16

Mongolia at a Turning-point

On Sunday, 2 April 1989, we stood for the last time on the platform of Ulan Bator's main railway station as the train from Moscow drew in. The sun was shining as brightly, the sky was as blue and the cold as intense as on our arrival two years previously. But whereas on our arrival the ambassadors and their wives had been lined up formally to welcome us, on the morning of our departure they and our embassy staff and Mongolian friends were ringed around us, reflecting the warm friendship and, indeed, affection that had grown out of shared experiences in a particularly unusual setting. We could not linger on the platform, because our heavy clothing and fur hats, which we would no longer need, had been packed away. We climbed aboard the train and were shown by the Chinese attendant to the usual quaintly old-fashioned de luxe cabin. The train lurched and then started to move forward. Frantic waving between us and our friends on the platform was curtailed as they were enveloped in clouds of steam from the train's heating. We tried to absorb as deeply as we could every last glimpse of Ulan Bator until it, too, was out of sight.

We settled down in our cabin on the thirty-hour journey to Beijing. From our window, I gazed at the sweep of Mongolia's empty vastness. But if it all looked much as it must have done in the days of Genghis Khan, the Mongolia I was leaving in 1989 had changed from the place I arrived in two years previously. The change was not as far-reaching as in the Soviet Union and some of the other socialist countries, but it was already significant and it was set to be progressive. If only . . .

The Mongolia I was looking back at in 1989 was itself still looking back at the Soviet Union. At that time no one, either in the West or the East, could foresee what would become of Mikhail Gorbachev and of reform in the Soviet Union. The Mongolians were certainly not the only people keeping their fingers crossed. Moreover, they had a very clear idea as to what effect a reversal in the Soviet Union would have on them.

Mongolia was no Eastern European country with bright beacons of Western Europe beckoning directly across its borders. There could be no sudden dash for freedom, such as the Hungarians and other Eastern

Europeans in 1989 looked like making. In any case, people like the Hungarians had a much clearer idea of the sort of freedom they wanted than the Mongolians, who were only just coming to realise that there could be such a thing as choice. However, more importantly, if the Mongolians' time for choice were to come, they would have to face up to new and difficult circumstances. It would be one thing to discard for good their submission to the Soviet Union, becoming in the process genuinely independent; it would be an entirely different matter to lose Soviet protection. Kublai Khan had been the last Mongol to prevail over the Chinese. With the passing of his Yuan dynasty, the Mongols had experienced centuries of harsh Chinese rule. The Mongolian People's Republic may have secured its recognition by the Kuomintang government in 1946, and this may have been accepted when China became a People's Republic. However, no country which, like Mongolia, has the sparsest of all populations in the world relative to its area could feel at ease with a large and powerful neighbour whose population is the very largest. All this would not necessarily be a matter of merely academic concern. There could well be potential for conflict where China's interests were concerned; yet, to develop its own economic potential, Mongolia would need businesslike relations with China.

During the long Sino–Soviet dispute the position for Mongolia had been clear-cut, but this area of tension was one which Gorbachev had particularly wished to reduce. In my time in Mongolia, some ten thousand Soviet troops had been withdrawn from Mongolia, and a much larger number was preparing to pull out. If this process continued, the time could yet come when there would be no Soviet military presence left in Mongolia. Not only would this leave Mongolia on its own, it would inevitably detract from the strategic value that Mongolia had had for the Soviet Union. Moreover, as that strategic value had accounted for at least part of the considerable Soviet aid to Mongolia, there were implications where the future level of Soviet assistance was concerned.

In a sense, the Soviet Union would be freeing itself of Mongolia as much as Mongolia would be gaining its genuine independence. In our trade contacts with the Mongolians we had already seen clear signs of their desire to broaden their trade relations. Mongolian trade had been almost completely with the Soviet Union and other Comecon countries, invariably on a soft-currency or straight exchange basis. It irked the Mongolians, for example, that their valuable cashmere wool, supplied on such terms, could end up in the GDR, which would sell the cashmere to a Western buyer and would then pocket the hard currency received. The other side of the coin was that the Soviet Union could reply that it was providing Mongolia with imports like oil on soft terms, which it too could sell for hard currency elsewhere. For all this, it was difficult to see that, as long as the cumbersome Comecon system lasted, Mongolia would feel free to opt out. But, in any case, Soviet involvement in Mongolia's development had led to a massive Mongolian debt to the Soviet Union, amounting to about five thousand roubles per head of Mongolia's population. The Soviet Union would hardly write off so large a debt. Moreover, Mongolia's difficulties in settling it would surely act as a disincentive to the Soviet Union regarding further advances. In other words, the Soviet Union would probably avoid increasing its economic involvement in Mongolia.

Regardless of the debt, Mongolia would not be able to turn its back on the Soviet Union. Setting aside the established levels of bilateral trade, Mongolia had the unchangeable handicap of being a landlocked country. Whether by air or rail (and road), Russia was the vital transport link for Mongolia, the most important route being the Trans-Siberian railway. But that railway was already under tremendous strain and it could not cope with future needs. This pointed to the necessity of Mongolia finding another route. There was only one: through China.

With its spur off the Trans-Siberian railway, Mongolia was already linked with Beijing and, therefore, to the Chinese railway network. Passenger train services had long flowed smoothly, and there had been some freighting to Mongolia via China. But although some agreement had been reached on the point, it would be important to the development of the Mongolian economy for regular freight services to operate to and from a Chinese port, like Tianjin. The Mongolians should be mindful that this would provide the Chinese with a specific pressure point. Political developments in China would be watched carefully by the Mongolians, just as the Chinese would watch the Mongolians' conduct where their interests were concerned.

This led back to those areas of change in which the Mongolians could be expected to advance quickly. First and foremost, whatever happened, there was bound to be a substantial religious revival. Buddhist monasteries and temples that became mere museums would reopen to worshippers, while those that were destroyed would surely be rebuilt, particularly in the case of the Mansjid monastery, if only to honour the thousands of lamas who were executed there. It was more difficult to say whether young men, educated as atheists, would show interest in becoming lamas.

Secondly, there would be a reflowering of Mongolian culture. English could eventually take over from Russian as the main foreign language taught in schools, but primarily there would be a new emphasis on the Mongolian language, particularly where the old script, literature and poetry were concerned.

This religious revival and reflourishing of Mongolian culture were surely inevitable. They would restore the Mongolians' self-respect and bolster their sense of independence. Revival of religion in Mongolia would be the revival of Tibetan-style Buddhism. The Mongolians would surely not court trouble with China, but nevertheless the Chinese could come to see a Buddhist revival in Mongolia as a beacon casting its light back on to Tibet, an autonomous region of China. Then, to a lesser extent, China could come to see a reflourishing of Mongolian culture and self-awareness in Mongolian as a threat to its hold over Inner Mongolia and Xinjiang.

Mongolia border trade with China had already restarted and was set to increase; and there had already been cultural and sporting exchanges with Inner Mongolia, which seemed likely to expand. But these were details. Mongolia's old problem looked like re-emerging – that is to say, any change in its relations with one of its two powerful neighbours automatically called for readjustment of its relations with the other powerful neighbour. If Mongolia disengaged from the Soviet Union it would have to plot its own new course where China was concerned, a China which, in contrast to the Soviet Union, was pursuing economic rather than political reform. China would remain unpredictable. The havoc wreaked in Inner Mongolia by the Cultural Revolution had sent shockwaves through Mongolia, and it should not be forgotten that for every one Mongolian in empty Mongolia there were over 500 Chinese in an overcrowded China. Yet for all that, China could be an important key to Mongolia's economic development, and if a relationship was to be established it was going to call for a great deal of careful management.

By 1989, there was at last a prospect of Mongolia being able to develop and benefit from new relations with Western countries and particularly Japan. Mongolia's situation as a distant and landlocked market would remain a distinct handicap. However, eventual Western assistance to Mongolia with a population of only two million could have a very significant impact. With up-to-date know-how, Mongolia could conceivably become an Asian New Zealand, producing meat for markets in the Far East. Production of valuable animal products, like cashmere wool and camel hair, could be increased, while Mongolia surely had untapped mineral wealth and, possibly, oil as well. If the Mongolians could cope with their debt to the Soviet Union and develop their chronic infrastructure, their country was not without economic promise.

Such, then, was the outlook in 1989 for Mongolia as it reached its momentous turning-point. But how did it all work out thereafter?

17

It Came to Pass

Three years have elapsed since I left Mongolia, three years spent in the totally different setting of the Seychelles. These beautiful islands in the Indian Ocean, a thousand miles from anywhere else, are remote from the hustle and bustle of the rest of the world. Yet even in this seclusion, one could not fail to be amazed by the momentous events which, in so short a time, have transformed so much in the world.

My diary records that, on leaving Mongolia, we spent only one night in Beijing. Two months later demonstrations for democracy filled the vast Tiananmen Square, and on the night of the 3–4 June Chinese troops fired on the crowds. The democracy movement in China was to be suppressed.

My diary also records, albeit far from comprehensively, the succession of some of the momentous events that followed over the next three years. Looking through this list – even though it is superficial – still brings back all the sheer amazement.

25 June 1989   Elections in Poland – Mazowiecki, the first non-Communist prime minister in Eastern Europe.

10 September 1989   The Hungarian government announced its willingness to allow GDR citizens to enter or leave Hungary through *any* border crossing point, and thereby opened the floodgates to the West for GDR citizens travelling via Hungary.

2 October 1989   Major demonstrations in Leipzig, five days before the GDR's fortieth anniversary.

9 November 1989   Opening of the Berlin Wall announced by the GDR.

24 November 1989   Mass demonstration in Prague – the hard-line leader Jakes fell.

22 December 1989   Revolt in Romania. Ceaucescu overthrown.

87

29 December 1989   Vaclav Havel took over as Czechoslovakia's non-Communist president.

2–3 October 1990   German unity – GDR ceased to exist.

20 December 1990   Schevardnadze resigned as Soviet Foreign Minister, and warned of plotting against reforms.

18 August 1991   *Coup* in the Soviet Union. Gorbachev removed from power.

21 August 1991   Failure of the *coup* in the Soviet Union. Gorbachev returned to Moscow, but Yeltsin the winner.

The overall connection between these events is perfectly clear. Aspirations, held far too long in check, built up an irresistible force which finally burst forth. It is easy to say that, at some stage, it was inevitable that this would happen. Nevertheless, the speed with which one event succeeded another bordered on the incredible. It took a Gorbachev, who came to power in May 1985, to set the scene; subsequently, momentum took over. The decision of the Hungarian government, in September 1989, to allow GDR citizens in Hungary to leave for the west if they wished to do so, was to act like a rocket-booster. The GDR would eventually have crumbled in any case, but the Hungarian decision speeded up the process. Then, when it was seen that the almost-model GDR was coming apart, the remaining entrenched Eastern European regimes toppled like ninepins. Against this background, it is striking that the Mongolian People's Revolutionary Party did not fall – although it was forced to yield its monopoly of power. By the end of 1990, it had retained a greater role in Mongolia than its Soviet counterpart could by then claim in the Soviet Union.

The brutality and personality cult had died with Choybalsan in 1952 – Mongolia was left with no Ceaucescu. Its own Brezhnev, Tsedenbal (who had wanted Mongolia to become the sixteenth republic of the Soviet Union) had been deposed in 1984. His successor Jambyn Batmonkh and his colleagues were not far-sighted reformers in themselves. However, although there were still some members of the old guard in their ranks, they took their cue from Gorbachev. In December 1988, a Central Committee plenum adopted a programme of political reform. Moreover, the forging of new trade links beyond the Council for Mutual Economic Assistance (the CMEA, or Comecon) was to be encouraged (because Gorbachev was urging Mongolia to look to new markets) and, particularly significantly, Mongolian national traditions were to be restored. Willy-nilly, the party had therefore stolen some of the opposition's clothes before an opposition had even come into being. However, *glasnost* (openness) subsequently made great strides, yet *perestroika* (restructuring) was barely discernible. In 1989, consumers grumbled about poor supplies, and complaints about pollution and Soviet exploitation of Mongolia's mineral wealth increased. Criticism was aired in the press, and there was a new tolerance of religion as well as a striking rebirth of Mongolian traditions and culture. But political reform was paltry, industry continued to creak on and animal husbandry still lagged behind its potential. Again, Batmonkh and his colleagues, who had not looked like real reformers, achieved quite inadequate political and economic reform.

The average age of the population being well under forty, there was a receptiveness to new ideas. It was at this stage that the various changes in Eastern Europe in the second half of 1989 had an effect in Mongolia, particularly on younger intellectuals in Ulan Bator. On 10 December 1989 the Mongolian Democratic Union was formed. The battle for a multi-party system with free elections, a market economy and human rights had begun. The ruling Mongolian People's Revolutionary Party responded by agreeing to a dialogue with the Democratic Union on reform, but otherwise tried to play it long. Popular demonstrations which had been held earlier, in the depths of winter, increased with hunger strikes applying particular pressure. After some prevarication, when the use of force against the demonstrators was considered but rejected, the entire ruling politburo resigned. Batmonkh was replaced as general secretary of the party by Gombojabyn Ochirbat. Then, at a meeting in March 1990 of the Great People's Hural, Punsalmaagiyn Ochirbat (a different Ochirbat) was chosen as chairman of the Hural and thereby became head of state. Gungaadorj, the minister of agriculture, became premier. Significantly, the Hural also agreed to revise the Constitution to adopt a presidential system, to end the leading role of the Communist party, and to bring in a multi-party system based on free elections.

By this time the opposition had organised into different political parties, though they lacked experience, resources and any real foothold in rural areas, a key factor because of their disproportionately larger number of constituencies. It was in such fields that the Mongolian People's Revolutionary Party sought to exploit its strength in the run-up to the first multi-party elections in Mongolia. However, complaints by opposition parties that the ruling party was exploiting unfair advantages were backed up by international pressure, and eventually the ruling party made concessions. The elections in July 1990, held under foreign supervision, resulted in the Mongolian People's Revolutionary Party winning just over 60 per cent of the votes as against the Mongolian

Democratic Party's 24 per cent, the Party of National Progress's just under 6 per cent and the Social Democratic Party's 5.5 per cent. The clear win by the Mongolian People's Revolutionary Party came as no surprise, although their performance in Ulan Bator was comparatively weak. Despite their victory, however, the party had the new experience of having to work with three opposition parties, the ratio of whose total seats in the new Small Hural was about two to the three of the Mongolian People's Revolutionary Party. On 4 September 1990 Punsalmaagiyn Ochirbat was elected President of Mongolia, and a Social Democrat, Gonchigdorj, was to be his Vice-President. The number of ministries was halved, and freedoms of the press, religion and foreign travel were guaranteed. At the postponed 20th Congress of the Mongolian People's Revolutionary Party in February 1991, the replacement of the other Ochirbat as general secretary by the younger Dashyondon implied that the party was to continue with reform. Mongolia was to cease being called a People's Republic, and democracy was to be enshrined in the Constitution. Meanwhile, laws covering foreign investment and privatisation had been passed. Moreover, somewhat similar to the Czechoslovak system, privatisation share vouchers were made available to every citizen of Mongolia. Prices were reformed and the tugrik was devalued to prepare for eventual full convertibility of the Mongolian currency. Mongolia had also joined the World Bank, the International Monetary Fund and the Asian Development Bank, and it was to have its own stock exchange.

For centuries the outside world had shown virtually no interest in Mongolia. All that changed from 1989 onwards. President Ochirbat visited the United States, having previously been in Britain. US Secretary of State James Baker visited Mongolia in July 1991, followed by Toshiki Kaifu, then Prime Minister of Japan. Other visitors included the Chinese head of state, Yang Shangkun, and – the Dalai Lama.

On the ground in Mongolia, however, life had become steadily more difficult. On a visit to Moscow in 1990, the two Ochirbats were unsuccessful in trying to persuade the Soviet government to cancel Mongolia's vast debt, although they managed to achieve some alleviation. Furthermore, the Soviet government was eventually obliged, in the face of its own problems, to cut back its oil supplies to Mongolia. One bright spot for the Mongolians was that, with the marked increase in the private ownership of cattle, the national herd reached the significant total of twenty-five million for the first time. Otherwise, serious inflation, a heavy budget deficit, rising unemployment and food shortages all made up a dismal picture. Rationing of essential food items was introduced as Mongolia started to experience the pain of the transition to a market economy.

In August 1991 the Mongolians benefited from a victory for which they did not have to fight, yet but for which they could have lost so much. The failure of the coup against Gorbachev surely had the consequence for the Mongolians of confirming their independence. Any question of Mongolia being dragged back into submission to Moscow had been settled once and for all as Moscow itself went on to change out of all recognition. But this still left the Mongolians in very difficult circumstances. If the former Soviet domination had ceased, so too had most of the assistance that went with it – yet the debt still remained. Even if the Mongolians had never heard of a curate's egg, by 1992 many of them believed that their new situation was partly good and partly bad. The good part was that they were well on the way to recovering their national identity (with, for example, the renaissance of Lamaism and the progress towards re-introduction of the old Mongolian script) as well as the new freedom of speech which was valued. But the bad seemed to be getting dispro-portionately worse. The old inefficient state-sector economy had ground to a halt. In such a vast country where in any case one-third of fuel supplies are consumed in delivery of the other two-thirds, worsening fuel shortages only made matters worse, particularly with power cuts and distribution breakdowns. Even meat and milk which the Mongolians themselves produced were in short supply, adding to a food shortage that was assuming crisis proportions. On top of all this, increasing prices, inflation and soaring unemployment, made many people start to long for their old economic system. Increasingly, this worked to the detriment of those opposition parties who were pressing the pace of change.

Responding to this pace, the Mongolian People's Revolutionary Party turned its back on (its own) Communism, and in February 1992 it went on to discard socialism as well. At that stage, the party considered dropping the 'Revolutionary' adjective from its name. It was decided, however, that in the run-up to the second general election in mid-1992 the old name would be more familiar to the electorate. As the election approached the party received substantial financial assistance from China, which led to opposition claims that the party was exchanging freedom for a bowl of rice. In the event, however, the Mongolian People's Revolutionary Party went on to win a landslide victory. In their changing world, which appeared to be one of the new-found economic hardship, many people were apparently attracted by the 'Revolutionary' familiar. This was a setback for the opposition, particularly for the Social Democrats. They were incensed that, although the People's Revolutionary Party had discarded all its former ideological heavy baggage, it nevertheless bore responsibility for the previous seventy years. Moreover, they claimed that the People's Revolutionary Party consisted of former Communists who had hijacked reform but who could not be expected to produce the progress to a successful market economy.

The opposition consists of a number of parties, ranging from those with special interests (like the Herdsmen and Peasants Party) to the Social Democrats. The latter attracts bright young intellectuals who drew inspiration from the changes in Eastern Europe. Some of them had also had glimpses of the outside world, particularly through programmes such as the English language courses at Leeds. But such intellectuals were centred mainly on Ulan Bator; for those Mongolians leading relatively simple lives in the vast country areas, the programmes of parties like the Social Democrats were, arguably, too sophisticated to make the impact that, in the first general election in July 1990, they had made in the capital. That the opposition (including the Social Democrats) lost ground even in the capital in the second general election in July 1992 was indeed a setback for them.

However, it does not follow that reform in Mongolia has been thwarted. Rather, it seems, the pace of change cannot be rushed. Having been schooled for so long in the belief that capitalism was a bad system (and never having had any direct experience of it anyway), it is a testing time for the Mongolians as they move towards a capitalist system and experience great transitional hardships in these early stages. A stock market in Mongolia is an amazing development in itself, but when set against the food shortages and power cuts it is not something that many Mongolians can yet understand, let alone see as relevant.

Otherwise, the Mongolians' situation is not unfavourable. Even though, outside the capital, the population is widely dispersed in a vast country, at merely two million its needs are manageable in a way that many developing countries would envy. Secondly, Mongolia is now receiving fairly substantial international aid which, in view of the small population, can have a considerable impact. Thirdly, Mongolia is not set to suffer the sort of racial conflicts that have broken out, one after another, in various parts of the former Communist world. In Mongolia, there has not been nor is there likely to be a Sarajevo or a Nagorno Karabakh.

18

Now it is Ulaanbaatar

If I were to return to Mongolia today it would no longer be a People's Republic, let alone the one that I knew between 1987 and 1989 (even though it was by then no longer the very harsh place that my predecessors experienced after our mission was first established in 1965). The name of the capital has not changed as I expected that it might. However, it is no longer appropriate to write Ulan Bator – which spelling in English was taken over from the Russian version. Now the Mongolian version, Ulaanbaatar, is the correct one.

In the Mongolian capital, Stalin's statue was eventually pulled down in February 1990. Moreover, Choybalsan has been recognised as the mass murderer of his own people that he was; also there were strident calls for Tsedenbal to be put on trial, but he died in exile in Moscow in April 1991. However, if former idols have understandably been reviled, the Mongolians have not only rehabilitated the previously unmentionable Genghis Khan, but have come close to making him a national symbol. Yet comparatively little has been said about Sühbaatar, the man who was attributed with having led the revolution in 1921. With his death in mysterious circumstances in 1923, when he was only thirty years of age, he was surely one of the first victims of the brutality that followed; it seems likely that eventual evaluation will confirm him as a Mongolian hero, even, maybe, a more fitting one than Genghis Khan.

The Mongolian Minister of Agriculture, who in 1987 was too scared to advise me as to which state farms I should visit, became prime minister in March 1990. I was not surprised to hear that, six months later, he was replaced. The jolly chairman of the then State Committee for External Economic Relations, who in 1988 made such a favourable impression on a visiting British trade mission and whom I always found particularly helpful as well as delightful company, became President of Mongolia.

However, the most far-reaching change has been that the Soviet Union itself ceased to exist as such. The deterioration had become so seemingly terminal that when the Soviet Union finally broke up, it came as no great

93

surprise. How far we have all come in such a short time! For so very long, and until the attempted *coup* in Moscow in August 1991, it was impossible to conceive of the Union of Soviet Socialist Republics simply ceasing to exist. How much more bewildering it must have been for the Mongolians who, for far longer than any other people, had followed a Soviet way of life. Soviet domination as well as Soviet assistance marked virtually every aspect of life in Mongolia, but now those long decades of shared experience and suffering have finally passed into history. The reality which now faces the Mongolians is that the passing of the Soviet Union has not simply confirmed the Mongolians' independence, it has made their responsibility for their own affairs a fact of life.

The original model of all Communist parties having disappeared together with the Soviet Union of its own creation, it is particularly striking that the Mongolian People's Revolutionary Party has managed to keep going at all, let alone to lead the country on the way out of its ideologically dominated and authoritarian past towards a market economy and multi-party democracy. At the outset the party did not resist reform, although its early efforts in that direction were at best half-hearted. As opposition parties developed, the People's Revolutionary Party prevaricated in an attempt to retain control, yet managed to reform itself just in time. By espousing the revival of Mongolian culture, religion and traditions (including the rehabilitation of Genghis Khan), the party secured the high ground where expression of nationalism was concerned. In July 1992 the party secured a landslide victory because the hardships of economic transition worked to the detriment of those opposition parties pressing for faster reform. After those elections, the People's Revolutionary Party shunned coalition, as, after their landslide victory, they had a right to do. However, the ruling party has a responsibility which goes far beyond the rehabilitation of Genghis Khan. With such a small population yet with relatively substantial outside aid, Mongolia can progress to a market economy – and it must do so. There will be no place for further prevarication or inertia. It remains to be seen whether the People's Revolutionary Party can rise to the occasion, or whether at a later stage the electorate will turn to the opposition. The immediate problem is to solve the food crisis, but that crisis does not detract from the fact that Mongolia has already come a long way. It is moving as fast as its people can accept, if not as fast as some of them would want.

Today, the uncertainties and, in some cases, the turmoil and bloody conflicts which have burst out in the aftermath of the break-up of the former Communist world are a matter of immediate concern to us all. Mongolia was one of the oldest parts of that world, and it faces the problems of fundamental readjustment that others are confronting. That it is doing so with relatively less experience and insight than others in the same boat, yet without causing bloodshed, floods of refugees or problems with unwanted babies and the like, is surely no mean feat. The country has a long way to go to reach its full potential but, when one looks back, it can be claimed that, already, Mongolia has come of age.

19

Tourism to Mongolia

Mongolia has often been regarded as a joke. It was supposed to be a joke when we, in Ulan Bator, received a telephone call from the host of a late-night party somewhere in London, one of whose guests had thoughts of loading the host's telephone bill by booking a call to Mongolia. The Mongolian operator, not unreasonably, decided to put the strange call, with its background sounds of guffaws and cork-popping, through to the British embassy. When we answered the call – announcing who we were and, more to the point, where we were – the host asked (albeit 'as a taxpayer') why on earth he should want to call Mongolia, as if it had all been our idea in the first place. Then, on one occasion, Mongolia was taken as a snub. A lady setting out by British Rail on her long journey to Ulan Bator was asked by a fellow-traveller where she was going. Her reply 'Mongolia', sounded so outlandish that it was taken as a sign that she did not wish to continue the conversation. The idea that Mongolia might be a real destination was somehow beyond grasp. But then, a few weeks earlier, we had received a letter addressed to us in Outer Magnolia – a part of *Gardeners' World*?

Of course, Mongolia is distant and remote. A sixty-minute hold-up in traffic on the M25 is not exactly an unusual experience, but on one occasion a traveller precisely so caught out had his travel connections utterly disrupted to the extent that he finally arrived in Ulan Bator eight days late. There are a number of reasons, some of which have already been touched on, as to why Mongolia's remoteness puts it seemingly beyond the real world. For long decades it was closed to the outside world, and even in comparatively recent times visitors to Mongolia were not welcome. But that changed. Initially the change was cautious and limited, and any foreign visitor thrusting a Bible or religious tract into uncomprehending Mongolian hands only served to convince the authorities that they were right to be cautious.

By the late 1980s, tourism from Western countries to Mongolia had already reached ten thousand a year, and this did not include a much larger number of rail travellers between Beijing and Moscow who passed through Mongolia without staying. Two hotels in the capital, the Bayangol and the Hotel Ulan Bator, provided accommodation for tourists (who, on days of an important Communist Party meeting, could be turfed out of the one and moved into the other to make room for fraternal delegates), and a third and much larger hotel has since been built. Outside the capital tourists could be accommodated, often in ger camps as has already been mentioned, at Terelj, at Dalandzadgad in the South Gobi and at Khujirt between the ancient capital Karakorum, with the nearby Erdene Dzuu monastery, and the Khukhreh Falls on the River Orhon. There were other camps and rest-houses in the *aimags* or provinces of Hovd, Arhangai, Hövsgöl, Govaltay and Hentiy, but arrangements to stay had to be made well in advance.

It is one thing to get off the beaten track in Europe. In Mongolia, most routes are literally beaten tracks – often several alongside each other as drivers have progressively sought to avoid fissures and potholes created by erosion. From the air, such multi-tracks look like the broad-front advance route taken by some armoured brigade; on the ground, such tracks can be very confusing, especially when they split up seemingly haphazardly. On one occasion we were driving across the Gobi Desert and, with no distinguishing feature let alone prominent landmark in sight, I noticed my driver scanning the horizon. He was clearly at a loss, yet he drove steadily on until, eventually, we came upon a line of telegraph poles which we were then able to follow to our destination. In that long drive we came across no one; and in the event of a breakdown or some other setback, it would have been strictly self-help. This brings out the point that fuel, food, accommodation and other facilities are thinly spread in the vastness of Mongolia's outback. Distances are great, areas in between are empty, the terrain is often hard and climatic conditions can be extreme. For such reasons, even after the passing of the Stalinist era when Mongolia was no longer off limits, applications by individuals and organisations to undertake their own camel treks or university expeditions and so forth were often turned down.

Such factors as the great distances, the hard terrain and the climate still apply; otherwise, there have been notable changes. In the first place, many tourists are in general looking for new and unusual destinations, and specialised and adventure tourism is making inroads into the old-style package holiday trade. Set alongside this, Mongolia has some appeal for general tourists and considerable attractions where specialised tourism is concerned. Fortunately, this coincides with a new Mongolian attitude. Tourism to Mongolia is surely set to increase, because the country's transition away from authoritarian Communism to democracy is making for a more open and relaxed attitude to the outside world – and also because the parallel conversion to a market economy depends on the maximising of hard-currency earnings from every possible source. However, the food and fuel shortages and the power cuts that the Mongolians are now experiencing must also be a handicap where tourism is concerned. With the transitional difficulties, tourism to Mongolia has yet to reach its potential. However, it is particularly encouraging that it has started to diversify, enabling visitors to follow special interests which formerly would have been unacceptable to the authorities. Hunting trips, often based on camps in remote areas, are now a regular feature, and there have been expeditions to trek in the Gobi, to climb peaks in the High Altai Mountains and to search for Genghis Khan's grave and so on. Mongolia also offers scope for a wide range of other special interests, such as angling, canoeing, exploration, archeology and geology.

Then, there are the flora and fauna. Despite claims that it is extinct in Mongolia, Przewalski's horse can apparently be seen, as can wild camels. From Siberian fox, snow leopard and reindeer in the north to Gobi bears and the strange saiga goat-like antelope, the animal life is very varied. More varied still is the birdlife (both resident and migratory), including hoopoe, Bewick swans, cranes, storks, bustards, cormorants, grouse, geese, partridge, kites, eagles, terns, skylarks, sandpipers and desert warblers. As for the spectacular flora, many of the flowers in European gardens grow wild in Mongolia, including iris, delphiniums, azaleas, columbines, poppies and lilies. Moreover, alpine flowers such as edelweiss, gentian and many types of saxifrage grow in much greater profusion than anywhere in the Alps, and in areas like the Gobi there are highly unusual varieties of plantlife.

With its 240 days a year of bright-blue skies and brilliant sunshine, Mongolia is invigorating whatever the climate, and there are no particular health hazards. Moreover, the landscape, which varies very considerably in so large a country, has a wonderful feel to it, conveying a sense that it goes on for ever, as one horizon opens on another.

Landlocked as Mongolia is, it can only be reached by rail or by air, via China or Russia. The weekly international express between Moscow and Beijing provides the main rail link, although slow trains operate more frequently to Ulan Bator from Beijing and Irkutsk. There are regular flights between Moscow and Ulan Bator and China Airways now operate scheduled flights from Beijing.

Mongolia is at its most beautiful from late May to mid-September, and this is roughly the season for outlying tent camps. Special arrangements are made for hunters during the colder months, but generally tourists should stick to the short summer season. At that time the daytime temperature can build up to 28°C (and higher in the Gobi), but the heat is comfortable in the dry air. Even during the fairly frequent summer rain showers, the humidity is low. Hours of summer daylight are roughly from five o'clock in the morning to ten at night, and all Mongolia operates on Greenwich Mean Time plus eight hours.

Mongolia will never become a fashionable destination for mass tourism, but there are now few places in the world where one can acquire such a sense of getting away from it all. It has to be admitted that this includes getting away from plush facilities that some would consider essential, but Mongolia is for the adventurous, and it and its people exert a very special and powerful charm on the visitor.

POSTSCRIPT

It was in a tropical climate that I was writing this book when, by chance, I received a letter from Mongolia. From its postmark, the letter had taken a year to arrive. Addressed to me, as it was, in 'Seychelles, Indian Ocean', the delay was perhaps understandable. But I could not account for the fact that the Christmas card and the letter inside the envelope were dated a whole year before the letter had been postmarked. There was no doubt that the letter was indeed two years old. In the first place, it was from the GDR ambassador, whose embassy had long since been taken over by the Federal Republic of Germany. Secondly, much of the letter was about changes yet to come, but which are now matters of history. In its way, the letter has served to remind me that so much has happened in the past few years, it all seems like a very long time ago.

By contrast, my memories of Mongolia remain as clear as the crystal waters of Lake Hövsgöl, as sharp as the taste of fresh camel's milk in the Gobi, yet as sweet as steppe honey. I can only come back to the words of Beatrix Bulstrode over seventy years ago:

'Mongolia fascinated me in anticipation; in materialisation; in retrospect; and most of all in the prospect of going back – some day.'